T0360732

"The question of what constitutes acceptable risk has always involved a judgement about both science and politics. This issue is brought into sharp focus in this volume about the changing relationship between science, novel risks and society. The contributors, drawn from academia and the world of government policy, show how this relationship is of critical importance for the ways we now think about trust in institutions and risk governance. The important message of the book is that while we have not yet reached a 'post-truth' world in decision-making about risks, we need to guard against such a situation happening in the future. A timely and welcome contribution to a critical contemporary societal debate."

Nick Pidgeon MBE, Professor and Director of the Understanding Risk Research Group, Cardiff University, UK

Risk and Uncertainty in a Post-Truth Society

This edited volume looks at whether it is possible to be more transparent about uncertainty in scientific evidence without undermining public understanding and trust.

With contributions from leading experts in the field, this book explores the communication of risk and decision-making in an increasingly post-truth world. Drawing on case studies from climate change to genetic testing, the authors argue for better quality evidence synthesis to cut through the noise and highlight the need for more structured public dialogue. For uncertainty in scientific evidence to be communicated effectively, they conclude that trustworthiness is vital: the data and methods underlying statistics must be transparent, valid, and sound, and the numbers need to demonstrate practical utility and add social value to people's lives.

Presenting a conceptual framework to help navigate the reader through the key social and scientific challenges of a post-truth era, this book will be of great relevance to students, scholars, and policymakers with an interest in risk analysis and communication.

Sander van der Linden is Assistant Professor of Social Psychology at the University of Cambridge, UK, where he directs the Cambridge Social Decision-Making Laboratory.

Ragnar E. Löfstedt is Professor of Risk Management at King's College London, UK, and Director of King's Centre for Risk Management.

Earthscan Risk in Society series

Edited by Ragnar E. Löfstedt, King's College London, UK

Protecting Seniors Against Environmental Disasters
From Hazards and Vulnerability to Prevention and Resilience
Michael R. Greenberg

Anthropology and Risk
Åsa Boholm

Explaining Risk Analysis
Protecting Health and the Environment
Michael R. Greenberg

Risk Conundrums
Solving Unsolvable Problems
Edited by Roger E. Kasperson

Siting Noxious Facilities
Integrating Location Economics and Risk Analysis to Protect
Environmental Health and Investments
Michael R. Greenberg

Moral Responsibility and Risk in Society
Examples from Emerging Technologies, Public Health and
Environment
Jessica Nihlén Fahlquist

Risk and Uncertainty in a Post-Truth Society
Edited by Sander van der Linden and Ragnar E. Löfstedt

For more information about this series, please visit: https://www.
routledge.com/Earthscan-Risk-in-Society/book-series/ERSS

Risk and Uncertainty in a Post-Truth Society

Edited by
Sander van der Linden
and Ragnar E. Löfstedt

LONDON AND NEW YORK

from Routledge

First published 2019
by Routledge
2 Park Square, Milton Park, Abingdon, Oxon OX14 4RN

and by Routledge
52 Vanderbilt Avenue, New York, NY 10017

Routledge is an imprint of the Taylor & Francis Group, an informa business

British Library Cataloguing-in-Publication Data
A catalogue record for this book is available from the British Library

Library of Congress Cataloging-in-Publication Data
A catalog record has been requested for this book

ISBN: 978-0-367-23543-7 (hbk)
ISBN: 978-0-429-28029-0 (ebk)

Typeset in Times New Roman
by codeMantra

Contents

Figures

Tables

Contributors

Ian L. Boyd is Chief Scientific Adviser at the Department of Environment, Food and Rural Affairs (DEFRA). He is currently Professor in Biology at the University of St Andrews. He has received the Scientific Medal of the Zoological Society of London and the Bruce Medal for his research in polar science. He is a Fellow of the Royal Society of Edinburgh and the Society of Biology. In 2017, Ian was awarded the prestigious Polar Medal.

Ed Humpherson is Director-General of Regulation at the UK Statistics Authority. He is the Authority's Principal Adviser on the assessment and reassessment of official statistics, and their compliance with the Code of Practice for Official Statistics. Prior to his current position, Ed was Director-General of Regulation, Board Member, and Executive Leader for Economic Affairs at the National Audit Office.

Sander van der Linden is Assistant Professor of Social Psychology at the University of Cambridge, where he directs the Cambridge Social Decision-Making Laboratory. He is also a Fellow of Churchill College, Cambridge, and Editor-in-Chief of the *Journal of Environmental Psychology*. He was named a Rising Star by the Association for Psychological Science and a recipient of the Frank Research prize in Public Interest Communications.

Ragnar E. Löfstedt is Professor of Risk Management at King's College London and Director of King's Centre for Risk Management. He is a Fellow of the Society for Risk Analysis (SRA), the Editor-in-Chief of the *Journal of Risk Research*, and Editor of the *Earthscan Risk in Society Series*. He received the Chauncey Starr Award for exceptional contributions to the field of risk analysis under the age of 40 from the SRA.

Geoffrey Podger is a Senior Visiting Research Fellow at King's College Centre for Risk Management. His current regulatory post is the Head of the UK Delegation to the Intergovernmental Commission on the Channel Tunnel. Previously, he was Chief Executive or equivalent successively of the UK Food Standards Agency, the European Food Safety Authority, the British Health and Safety Executive, and WorkSafe New Zealand.

David J. Spiegelhalter is the Winton Professor for the Public Understanding of Risk in the Statistical Laboratory, Centre for Mathematical Sciences, University of Cambridge. He is also President of the Royal Statistical Society (RSS), a Fellow of the Royal Society (FRS), and Chairman of the Winton Centre for Risk and Evidence Communication in the Department of Pure Mathematics and Mathematical Statistics at the University of Cambridge.

Emma Woods is Head of Policy at the Royal Society, the UK's national academy of science. She leads the Society's work on the well-being of living systems, convening expertise and providing policy advice on everything from UK agriculture to international biodiversity to human genome editing. She is also a Fellow of the Westminster Abbey Institute and a Policy Fellow at the Centre for Science and Policy (CSaP), University of Cambridge.

Foreword

Reading this inspiring volume, I had the feeling that none of its contributors endorsed its dispiriting title. However, they were deeply aware of the spectre of a post-truth society. As public servants, in official and unofficial posts, they have all been at the front lines of communicating with diverse, dispersed, and sometimes disinterested parties about research results that are unfamiliar, uncertain, and sometimes unwelcome.

The common thread in their reports is the need to create the conditions found in mutually respectful interpersonal discourse: a sustained two-way process, focussed on topics of common interest, using terms with shared meaning. Such discourse can avoid needless disagreements, arising from unintended slights and unwitting misunderstandings. The result should be fewer, but better conflicts.

In personal relations, such discourse requires knowing one's partners, the issues that concern them, and how they speak. The authors describe strategies for achieving those conditions when communicating on behalf of a formal organization or a diffuse body of scientific knowledge.

Their strategies have many elements of risk communication research. They begin by assembling the evidence relevant to the decisions facing all parties with a need to know. They continue by identifying the most critical evidence and characterizing its responsibility in terms of the uncertainty surrounding it and the pedigree of the science producing it. They then render that evidence as clearly as possible and disseminate it to as broad an audience as will listen.

However, demonstrating that they know their partners does not guarantee that their partners will know them. Fear about being misunderstood suffuses this volume. Some of that fear has benign sources. Without the duty to understand that public servants bear, other parties may rely on their intuitions regarding what scientists and public officials do, know, and want. Other fear has more malign sources. Parties who are displeased with the evidence may find it easier to impugn its bearers than to provide their own.

These enemies' work is made easier by the failings of public servants' own institutions. Rogue scientists can undermine the integrity of their colleagues. Consensus processes and lawyers can burden documents with useless detail and legalese, hiding essential information in plain sight. Complex, or dithering, decision-making processes can leave little time for the testing that all messages need. Administrative procedures can preclude the frank exchanges needed to clarify concerns and terms.

The authors have done their bit to reform their institutions. They cannot stop the noise surrounding uncertain evidence. However, they can offer a clear signal about their own identity. They are not politicians or publicists willing to distort the evidence. They are not lawyers or legal scholars accustomed to assembling the evidence supporting a position. They are public servants, committed to representing science, with its imperfect evidence and practices.

Individually, these chapters offer lessons that can win some battles by avoiding pitfalls that the authors have learned, sometimes through hard personal experience. Collectively, these chapters offer a strategy that can reduce the risk of losing the war: do not take the bait offered by science's enemies and act out of character, like partisans. People who do not remember what scientists and public officials said will remember whether they acted with dignity and respect. Despite the turmoil, science remains among our most trusted institutions. The present authors set the standard for keeping it that way.

Baruch Fischhoff
Pittsburgh, PA

Introduction

Risk and uncertainty in a post-truth society

Sander van der Linden and Ragnar E. Löfstedt

Like all good stories, this one started in a pub, in Princeton, NJ, where Ragnar and I first discussed the idea and need for a new conference and edited book dedicated to risk and decision-making under uncertainty in an increasingly "post-truth" world. Indeed, how to effectively manage societal risks and communicate uncertainty to the public about contested scientific evidence—without undermining trust—has proven to be an urgent and highly topical subject with important implications for public policy. Accordingly, the inaugural Risk and Uncertainty Conference (RUC) was held June 12–14, 2017 in Cambridge around the following theme: "*trust and evidence-based uncertainty communication in a post-truth society*". The aim of the conference was to bring together world-leading scholars on risk and uncertainty communication to help define and set an agenda for the field. Interest in the conference exceeded our expectations, and we are grateful to all of the attendees and keynote speakers that made the conference a tremendous success, including our sponsors; The Society for Risk Analysis (RSA), The Economic and Social Research Council (ESRC), The Winton Centre for Risk and Evidence Communication, King's College, London, and Churchill College, Cambridge. This edited volume represents timely and cutting-edge perspectives from our keynote speakers on the issue of risk and uncertainty communication. All contributors to this book occupy highly policy-relevant positions, ranging from the President of the Royal Statistical Society to the Director-General of the UK Statistics Authority to the Chief Scientific Adviser at the Department of Environment, Food, and Rural Affairs (DEFRA) to the Head of Policy at the Royal Society and the former Chief Executive of the European Food and Safety Authority (EFSA).

In the first chapter, David Spiegelhalter broadly outlines the lay of the land by tackling two key themes, the reproducibility crisis in science, and claims about post-truth and alternative facts, and how these two issues interact in complex ways with the communication of uncertainty to reduce trust in expertise, numbers, and science. In his role as statistician, risk communicator, and president of the Royal Statistical Society, David offers an important perspective on the root causes of the reproducibility crisis, as well as a conceptual framework to help navigate the reader through the key social and scientific challenges that lie ahead. In order to effectively communicate uncertainty about scientific evidence in a post-truth world, David concludes that gaining and maintaining trustworthiness is key. In Chapter 2, Emma Woods offers a deep dive into the world of science policy and notes how the post-truth era "ups the ante" for the role of evidence in society. Importantly, drawing on examples from climate change to genetic technologies, Emma outlines two key remedies: the need for better quality "evidence synthesis" to cut through the noise and an increased need for more structured public dialogue. As Head of Policy at the Royal Society, Emma brings a unique perspective to bear on these issues and sees the post-truth challenge as an opportunity to create a more robust and transparent role for science in policy-making. As Director-General of the UK's Statistics Authority, Ed Humpherson is faced with a considerable responsibility: regulating official statistics. Importantly, in Chapter 4, Ed speaks to the social relevance of statistics and highlights three core pillars needed for the effective management and communication of risk and uncertainty: trustworthiness, quality, and value. In other words, individuals and organizations need to demonstrate trustworthiness, the data and methods underlying statistics must be transparent, valid, and sound, and the numbers need to demonstrate practical utility and add social value to people's lives. The last two chapters deal with how risks and uncertainty emerge in government decision-making specifically and how they are managed in practice. Ian Boyd, Chief Scientific Advisor at DEFRA, notes that the concept of risk in government is often a social construct, where the perception of risk changes more so than the existence of the risk itself. Ian goes on to note that the process of risk management is highly dynamic and offers an insightful framework for thinking about governmental risk and decision-making under uncertainty from a complex systems perspective, focussing particularly on viable decision-making strategies in situations characterized by high risk and uncertainty. In the final chapter, Geoffrey Podger shares his experience as Chief Executive of the Foods Standard Agency and the European Food and Safety Authority, expressing serious concern over EFSA's new guidance on uncertainty in scientific assessment. Although the aim is to introduce a more transparent way of accounting for limitations in scientific knowledge, Podger notes the inherent difficulties with increasing transparency through a 200 page document. Considering earlier insights about the need for public dialogue and demonstrating trustworthiness, Podger ties it all together by asking whether such efforts really benefit the man on the street, whom ultimately, all regulators aim to serve. Returning to the original question that motivated the conception of this book: can we be more transparent about uncertainty in scientific evidence without undermining public understanding and trust? We hope that readers from all strands are well served by the timely and authoritative perspectives offered in this edited volume.

1 Trust in numbers[1]

David J. Spiegelhalter

Introduction

This chapter gives me a fine opportunity to bring together two topical issues. First, the claims of a reproducibility crisis in science, which have led to concerns about the quality and reliability of at least parts of the scientific literature; second, the suggestion that we live in a 'post-truth' society abounding in fake news and alternative facts, in which emotional responses dominate evidence-informed judgement. These two topics have a close connection: both are associated with claims of a decrease in trust in expertise, and both concern the use of numbers and scientific evidence. They are therefore of vital importance to professional statisticians or any who analyze and interpret data.

A simple Internet search will reveal the daunting amount that has been written about these contested issues, and here I can only give a brief personal review of the evidence and the possible causes, focussing on the 'filters' that distort statistical evidence as it is passed through the information pipeline from the originators to its final consumption by the public. No single group can deal with these complex matters, but I shall argue that statisticians, and in particular the Royal Statistical Society (RSS), have an essential role both in improving the trustworthiness of statistical evidence as it flows through the pipeline and in improving the ability of audiences to assess that trustworthiness. On statistical shoulders rests a great responsibility.

Reproducibility and replication

The idea of a 'reproducibility/replication crisis' might reasonably be said to date from John Ioannidis's 2005 article, which notoriously proclaimed '*Why most published research findings are false*' (Ioannidis 2005). Although initially concerned with the biomedical literature, the idea has since been applied particularly to psychology and other social sciences. (Note that although attempts have been made to define 'reproducibility' and 'replication' precisely (Leek & Jager 2017), I feel we should try to avoid giving yet more technical definitions to words in routine use[2]. So, I will treat the terms interchangeably and distinguish when an entire study is repeated or when data is re-analyzed).

The extent of this 'crisis' is contested. Ioannidis's initial article was based on modelling rather than empirical evidence: he argued that reasonable assumptions about the design of studies, biases in conduct, selection in reporting, and the proportion of hypotheses investigated that were truly non-null meant a high rate of 'false discoveries', i.e., the proportion of published positive results that were actually null hypotheses that had been falsely rejected. In contrast, an analysis of published *p*-values (Jager & Leek 2014) came up with an estimated false-discovery rate of 14 per cent in the mainstream medical literature, and a recent review (Leek & Jager 2017) concluded, '*We do not believe science is in the midst of a crisis of reproducibility, replicability, and false discoveries*'.

So, was the claim about false claims itself a false claim? This is strongly disputed by Ioannidis (2014) and, in a recent exercise Szucs and Ioannidis (2017), scraped nearly 30,000 *t* statistics and degrees of freedom from recent psychology and neuroscience journals; and on the basis of the observed effect sizes and low power, concluded, '*Assuming a realistic range of prior probabilities for null hypotheses, false report probability is likely to exceed 50% for the whole literature*'. Some of this apparent disagreement will be due to different literatures: Jager and Leek (2014) examined abstracts from top medical journals with many randomised controlled trials and meta-analyses, which would be expected to be much more reliable than first claims of 'discoveries'. And even a 14 per cent false-discovery rate might be considered too high.

An alternative approach is purely empirical, in which the experiments behind past published claims are replicated by other teams of researchers: for example the effect of 'power posing', popularised in a TED talk that has been viewed over 40 million times (Cuddy 2012), has been subject to repeated failed replications (Ranehill et al. 2015). The Reproducibility Project was a major exercise in which 100 psychology studies were replicated with higher power (Open Science Collaboration 2015): whereas 97 per cent of the original studies had statistically significant results, only 36 per cent of the replications did. This was widely reported as meaning that the majority of the original studies were false discoveries, but Patil (Patil, Peng & Leek 2016) pointed out that 77 per cent of the new results lay within a 95 per cent predictive interval from the original study, which corresponds to there not being a significant difference between the original and replication studies. This illustrates that the *difference between significant and not significant is often not significant* (Gelman & Stern 2006). But it also means that 23 per cent of original and replication studies had significantly different results.

Perhaps the main lesson is that we should stop thinking in terms of significant or not significant as determining a 'discovery', and instead focus on effect sizes. The Reproducibility Project found that replication effects were on average in the same direction as the originals but were around half their magnitude (Open Science Collaboration 2015). This clearly displays the biased nature of published estimates in their literature and strong evidence for what might be termed regression-to-the-null.

What's the cause of this 'crisis'?

It's important to note that deliberate fabrications of data do occur but appear relatively rare. A review estimated that 2 per cent of scientists admitted falsification of data (Fanelli 2009), and the US National Science Foundation and Office of Research Integrity deal with a fairly small number of deliberately dishonest acts (Mervis 2017), although substantial numbers of cases must go undetected as it is generally difficult to check raw material. Computational errors are more common but can be detected by repeating analyses if the original data is available.

Rather than deliberate dishonesty or computational incompetence, the main blame has been firmly placed on a *'failure to adhere to good scientific practice and the desperation to publish or perish'* (Begley & Ioannidis 2015). The crucial issue is the quality of what is submitted to journals, and the quality of what is accepted, and deficits are a product of what have become known as 'questionable research practices' (QRPs).

Figure 1.1 shows the results of a survey of academic psychologists in the US, which had a 36 per cent response rate (John, Loewenstein & Prelec 2012). A very low proportion admitted falsification, but other practices that can severely bias outcomes were not only frequently acknowledged but generally seen as defensible: for example the 50 per cent who admitted selectively reporting studies gave an average score of 1.66 when asked whether this practice was defensible, where $0 = $ no, $1 = $ possibly, and $2 = $ yes. An Italian survey found similar rates, although the respondents were more inclined to agree that the practices were not defensible (Agnoli et al. 2017).

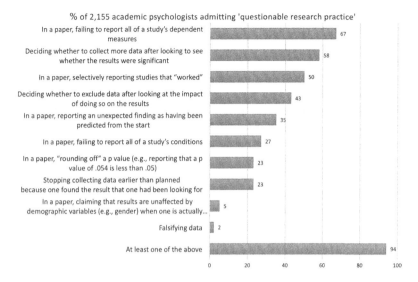

Figure 1.1 'Questionable research practices' (QRPs) admitted by 2,155 US academic psychologists (John, Loewenstein & Prelec 2012).

These QRPs just involve experimentation. If we consider general observational biomedical studies and surveys, then there are a vast range of additional potential sources of bias: these might include

- Sampling things that are convenient rather than appropriate.
- Leading questions or misleading wording.
- Inability to properly adjust for confounders and make fair comparisons.
- Too small a sample.
- Inappropriate assumptions in a model.
- Inappropriate statistical analysis.

And to these we might add many additional questionable practices concerned with interpretation and communication, which we shall return to later.

These are not just technical issues of, say, lack of adjustment of *p*-values for multiple testing. Many of the problems arise through more informal choices made throughout the research process in response to the data: say in selecting the measures to emphasize, choice of adjusting variables, cut-points to categorize continuous quantities, and so on; this has been described as the 'garden of forking paths' (Gelman & Loken 2014) or 'researcher degrees of freedom' (Simmons, Nelson & Simonsohn 2011) and will often take place with no awareness that these are QRPs.

There have been strong arguments that the cult of p-values is fundamental to problems of reproducibility, and recent guidance from the American Statistical Association clearly revealed their misuse (Wasserstein & Lazar 2016). Discussants called for their replacement or at least downplaying their pivotal role in delineating 'discoveries' through the use of arbitrary thresholds. We've already seen that p-values are fragile things that need handling carefully in replication studies – for example a study with $p = 0.05$ would only be predicted a 50 per cent chance of getting $p < 0.05$ in a precise replication.

This is a complex issue, and in a recent article (Matthews, Wasserstein & Spiegelhalter 2017) I confessed that I liked p-values, that they are good and useful measures of compatibility between data and hypotheses, but there is insufficient distinction made between their informal use in exploratory analysis and their more formal use in confirmatory analyses that summarise the totality of evidence – perhaps they should be distinguished as p_{exp} and p_{con}.

Essentially there is too strong a tendency to use p-values to jump from selected data to a claim about the strength of evidence to conclusions about the practical importance of the research. P-values do what they say on the tin, but people don't read the tin.

What gets into the scientific literature?

Questionable practices influence what is submitted to the scientific literature, and what finally appears depends on the publisher's ability to critique and select from what is presented to them. Ideally, peer review would weed out inadequate research and reporting, and recommend publication of good science, regardless of the actual results. But we know that peer review is often inadequate, and there is an urge for the leading journals, to a varying amount across different disciplines, to publish newsworthy, positive 'discoveries' and hence produce a skewed resource.

We should not be surprised at this since traditionally journals were set up to report new findings rather than the totality of evidence. Now there is an explosion in the amount of research and publishing opportunities; I would agree that '*most scientific papers have a lot more noise than is usually believed, that statistically significant results go in the wrong direction far more than 5% of the time, and that most published claims are overestimated, sometimes by a lot*' (Gelman 2013). Although

Gelman adds, more positively, that even though there are identifiable problems with individual papers, areas of science could still be moving generally in the right direction.

So, what can be done? A group of prominent researchers recently published a 'manifesto for reproducible science' whose recommendations for action are summarised in Table 1.1, together with the relevant stakeholders (Munafò et al. 2017).

This list demonstrates the responsibility of a wide range of stakeholders and is firm in its commitment to transparency. Statistical science has a major role in many of these proposals, in particular in methodological training, improving reporting and peer review, and sharing of data for re-analysis. However the one important element that seems to be missing from Table 1.1 is the need for external commentary, critique, and 'calling-out' of poor practice, which is the responsibility of the entire scientific community, the media, and the public – we shall return to this theme later.

In spite of extensive discussion about problems in the reliability of published science, these concerns do not seem to have yet fed into public opinion. A recent survey (Wellcome Trust 2017) revealed the trust ratings shown in Table 1.2.

It is ironic that pharmaceutical scientists are given low levels of trust, in spite of them working under far greater constraints than university scientists in terms of pre-specification of design and analyses for regulators, and arguably producing more trustworthy analyses (personally I would

Table 1.1 Proposals from the 'manifesto for reproducible science' (Munafò et al. 2017)

Theme	Proposal	Stakeholders
Methods	Protecting against cognitive biases	Journals, funders
	Improving methodological training	Funders, institutions
	Independent methodological support	Funders
	Collaboration and team science	Funders, institutions
Reporting and dissemination	Promoting study pre-registration	Journals, funders
	Improving the quality of reporting	Journals
	Protecting against conflicts of interest	Journals
Reproducibility	Encouraging transparency and open science	Journals, funders, regulators
Evaluation	Diversifying peer review	Journals
Incentives	Rewarding open and reproducible practices	Journals, funders, institutions

Table 1.2 Who is trusted as a source of medical research information?
Responses from 1,500 UK adults (Wellcome Trust 2017)

Profession	Trust completely or a great deal (per cent)	Trust very little or not at all (per cent)
Doctors or nurses	64	6
University scientists	59	4
Medical research charities	37	11
Pharma scientists	32	16
Industry scientists	29	16
Journalists	3	59

trust the opinion of pharma statisticians on medical research far more than that of many health professionals). Journalists are given very low trust ratings in spite of being a major source of information to the public.

This introduces the idea that expressions of trust are not, in general, based on careful consideration of evidence but arise as an immediate response based on our gut feelings, which brings us naturally to the way we handle all the other numbers that deluge us as part of daily life, and in particular those that appear on the news.

Numbers in the news

Scientists are not the only people reporting claims based on statistical evidence. Politicians, nongovernmental organizations (NGOs), and many other bodies are all competing for our attention, using numbers and science to provide an apparently 'objective' basis for their assertions. Technology has changed, encouraging an increasing diversity of sources to use online and social media to communicate, with few controls to ensure the reliable use of evidence. This has led to suggestions that we are in a time of populist political discourse in which appeals to our emotion triumph over reason.

At the extreme, there are completely fabricated, demonstrably false facts that can be honestly labelled 'fake news'. But as with science, I believe that deliberate fabrication is not the main issue; this will be better dealt with in the future by a combination of calling-out by fact-checking organisations such as Full Fact (2017), crowd-sourcing on social media, automatic algorithms, and possible regulation of social media sites: for example, Full Fact are covering the current election campaign in the *Evening Standard* as well as collaborating with Facebook on prominent advertising of 'Tips for spotting false news'.

As with science, a much bigger risk is manipulation and exaggeration through inappropriate interpretation of 'facts' that may be technically correct but are distorted by what we might call 'questionable interpretation and communication practices' (QICPs). Figure 1.2 provides a highly simplified view of the process by which we hear about statistical evidence as the end of a pipeline that starts with the originators of the data and then goes through the 'authorities', then through their press and communication offices to the traditional media, and finally to us as individual members of society.

The questionable practices adopted by some of the more ruthless press offices, communications teams, and journalists include those in Table 1.3.

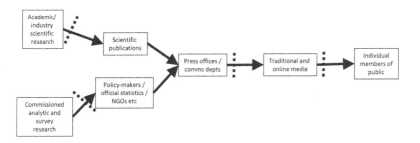

Figure 1.2 A simplistic diagram of the traditional information flows from statistical sources through to the public. The dashed lines indicate filters arising from questionable research, interpretation and communication practices (QRPs and QICPs), such as selective reporting, lack of context, and exaggeration of importance.

Table 1.3 Some highly questionable interpretation and communication practices (QICPs)

---

1 Pick stories that go against current consensus
2 Promote stories regardless of research quality
3 Don't report uncertainties
4 Don't provide context or comparative perspective, such as a time series
5 Suggest a cause when only an association is observed.
6 Exaggerate relevance and importance of findings
7 Claim the evidence supports a particular policy
8 Only provide relative and not absolute risks
9 Use positive or negative framing depending on whether aim is to reassure or frighten
10 Don't dwell on conflicts of interest or alternative views
11 Use a sexy but uninformative graphic
12 Write a headline which may have little connection to the story but will encourage clicks

---

Many of these would be seen as defensible by those whose professional career depends on attracting readers, listeners, or clicks, and it would be very interesting to conduct a survey of press officers and journalists to see how many of these they had used. But it is important to note that scientists might use these as well – in my personal experience some can, in spite of their proclaimed caveats, be too quick to jump to the wider implications of their work. When communicating subtle statistical evidence there seems an irresistible tendency to produce a simplifying narrative; we've seen X, it's because of Y, and so we should do Z.

This pipeline suggests it is too easy to blame journalists for misreporting science. Press offices, and the journals and scientists themselves, can be to blame; a recent study found that of 462 press releases from UK universities in 2011, 40 per cent contained exaggerated advice, 33 per cent contained exaggerated causal claims, and 36 per cent contained exaggerated inference to humans from animal research, and that the majority of exaggerations appearing in the press could be traced back to the press release (Sumner et al. 2014). The same team found slightly more reassuring results in 534 press releases from major biomedical journals: causal claims or advice in a paper were exaggerated in 21 per cent of corresponding press releases, although these exaggerations, which tended to be reported, did not produce more press coverage (Sumner et al. 2016).

One of my favourite examples of imaginative story-telling by a communications team is when a rather dull study, which found that 10 per cent of people carried a gene which protected them against high blood pressure (Newton-Cheh et al. 2009), was reframed negatively as nine in ten people carrying a gene which *increases* the risk of high blood pressure: this duly received international press coverage (Devlin 2009).

Another recent classic was a careful Swedish population study, whose published abstract (Khanolkar et al. 2016) said, '*We observed consistent associations between higher socio-economic position and higher risk of glioma*'; the press release headlined with '*High levels of education linked to heightened brain tumour risk*' (Medical Xpress 2016), and the sub-editor of the *Daily Mirror* finally turned it into '*Why going to university increases risk of getting a brain tumour*' (Gregory 2017).

The use of relative risks without absolute risks is a standard complaint and is explicitly warned against in British Broadcasting Corporation (BBC) statistical guidelines (BBC 2017). It is known that relative risks, often referred to by the media as simply an 'increased risk', regardless of magnitude, are an effective way of making a story look more exciting, and this is not helped by the fact that odds, rate, and hazard ratios are the standard output from most biomedical studies. The gripping headline '*Why binge watching your TV box sets could kill you*' (Donnelly 2016) arose from an epidemiological study that estimated an adjusted hazard ratio of 2.5 for a fatal pulmonary embolism associated with watching more than 5 hours TV a night compared with less than 2.5 hours (Shirakawa et al. 2016). But careful scrutiny of the absolute rate in the high risk group (13 in 158,000 person-years) could be translated as meaning you can expect to watch more than 5 hours TV a night for 12,000 years before experience the event, which somewhat lessens the impact. The newspaper article was, as usual, much better than the headline, but whose fault is it not to insist on including this *perspective*: the journalist, the press office, the publication, or the scientists?

I am unsure if this misuse of statistical evidence is getting worse. There are certainly more outlets promoting partial news, but mainstream websites, newspapers, and TV are perhaps under more scrutiny. What would fact-checkers have found were they active, say, 30 years ago? My unsupported feeling is that it would have been even worse than now.

But in my darkest moods I follow what could be called the 'Groucho principle': because stories have gone through so many filters that encourage distortion and selection, the very fact that I am hearing a claim based on statistics is reason to disbelieve it.

Trust in expertise

When faced with stories about how the natural world or society works, we can rarely check them for ourselves. So, *trust* is an inevitable element in dealing with statistical evidence, and therefore recent claims that there has been a decrease in trust in expertise are worth serious attention.

This claim is often associated with Michael Gove in the Brexit campaign saying that people have had enough of experts, but it is important to quote him in full: '*people have had enough of experts from organisations with acronyms saying that they know what is best and getting it consistently wrong' (YouTube 2016)*. This sounds a bit more reasonable and reflects recent high-profile failures to predict and control financial markets, and the lamentable quality of many political forecasts identified by the Good Judgement Project (Tetlock & Gardner 2015).

The evidence for such a decline is mixed. The Edelman Trust Barometer claims that 'trust is in crisis', and their poll shows that a 'person like yourself' is now as credible as a technical expert, yet their data show an overall increase in trust in government, the media, business, and NGOs since 2012 (Edelman 2017). A recent YouGov poll shows scientists trusted by 71 per cent, although this is 63 per cent vs. 83 per cent, depending on whether voting to leave or remain in the EU, and scientists come fourth in a UK trust league table behind nurses, doctors, and your own General Practitioner (YouGov 2017). Levels of trust in official statistics remain high and have increased (NATCEN Social Research 2017): of those able to give an opinion in 2016,

- 90 per cent trust Office for National Statistics (ONS).
- 85 per cent trust the statistics produced by ONS.
- 78 per cent agree that official figures are accurate.
- 26 per cent agree that government presents official figures honestly.
- 18 per cent agree that newspapers present official figures honestly.

These figures look reassuring to official statistics, although not to government or the media, but might improve further if pre-release access of politicians and their advisors to official statistics is abolished, an object of a continuing RSS campaign[3].

In her Reith lectures, philosopher Onora O'Neill points out the undifferentiated nature of these questions about who we trust and perhaps reflects a more general mood of suspicion (O'Neill 2002). More important is *active* trust, judged by our actions, which display that we commonly put our trust in institutions we profess not to trust. Crucially, she goes on to say that nobody can just expect to be trusted – they need to demonstrate *trustworthiness*.

Improving trustworthiness

In a remarkable TED talk (O'Neill 2013), Onora O'Neill argues that, rather than aiming to build trust, the task should be to become trustworthy – this means demonstrating competence, honesty, and reliability. But you also have to provide usable evidence that allows others to check whether you are trustworthy, which necessitates making yourself vulnerable to the other party. Although identifying *deception* as a key breaker of trust, she emphasises the danger of too much focus on policing deliberate fraud – this is too low a bar. This reinforces the need to avoid excessive attention to deliberate dishonesty, say, through data fabrication or demonstrably fake news, because it could distract attention from the more pressing problem of misleading, incompetent, and unreliable use of evidence.

There seem to be three main ways of building more trustworthiness in the statistical evidence pipeline shown in Figure 1.2: change the communication structure, improve the filters for the information being passed, and improve the ability of audiences to check trustworthiness.

Changing the communication structure

There are increasing possibilities to bypass potentially distorting filters. These include direct-to-public communication through social media by scientists, agencies, statistical 'experts', and even US presidents. While these innovations open up exciting opportunities for direct communication, there is also the risk of bypassing filters that have a positive role in weeding out poor science and statistics, and this emphasises even more the need for audiences to be able to appraise the reliability of what is being claimed.

Improving the filters

We've already seen the proposals in Table 1.1 for improving the reproducibility, and hence the trustworthiness, of published science. Many of these are concerned with transparency, but O'Neill has observed that transparency does not necessarily avoid deception (O'Neill 2002). She recommends 'intelligent transparency', which requires information to be 'accessible, intelligible, assessable, and useable' (Royal Society 2012). The crucial element is that audiences need to be able to inquire and not just accept assurances on trust.

Many of the ideas listed in Table 1.1 would also serve to improve trustworthiness in evidence in general, such as training of professionals, improved reporting standards, openness, and protection against conflicts of interest. Other measures that could enhance the reputation of scientific and statistical expertise might include clear demonstration of:

- *Uncertainty*: Many have recommended a greater willingness to embrace uncertainty (Makri 2017) and display humility (Shafik 2017). I would strongly concur but would add that this does not mean a reluctance to speak out confidently when faced with clear false statements or beliefs; perhaps we need a form of *muscular uncertainty*.
- *Engagement*: It seems essential to have empathy with audiences, and in particular understanding of their beliefs and concerns. As we shall see below, this can also allow some pre-emption of misunderstandings.

- *Impartiality*: Trustworthiness can be demonstrated by meticulous avoidance of broader agendas so that there is a clear demarcation between the description of the evidence and any potential policy recommendations. If scientists and statisticians are seen as advocates, then they must expect their objectivity to be questioned.

This final point is especially relevant to the history of the RSS, whose founding principles in 1834 included the pious assertion that

> The Statistical Society will consider it to be the first and most essential rule of its conduct to exclude carefully all opinions from its transactions and publications – to confine its attention rigorously to facts – and, as far as it may be found possible, to facts which can be stated numerically and arranged in tables.

This 'essential rule' was immediately ignored by fellows who made bold recommendations on the basis of flimsy data. Even contemporary commentators commented on the ambiguity of the term 'facts' (McConway 2016), with its implication of unquestionable veracity and authority, whereas data does not exist in a vacuum and only acquires meaning and value in a context.

This means acknowledging that numbers do not speak for themselves and so entails a responsibility to provide interpretation and potential implications of data, without slipping into advocacy or suggesting that the evidence mandates a particular decision without taking account of more general societal values. The current RSS strapline – *Data, evidence, decisions* – explicitly recognizes the role of statistical science at all stages of this path: for example the RSS's Data Manifesto encourages the publication of the evidence behind policies (Royal Statistical Society 2016) to 'show the working'. Interpretation can be provided in a clearly separate section of a report, as practiced by the Office for National Statistics.

When it comes to the specific outputs from press offices and the media, the primary aim should be to avoid the sort of questionable communication practices listed in Table 1.3. This might be helped by

- Construction and adoption of reporting guidelines, such as the simple list commissioned by the Levesen Inquiry (Fox 2012). The RSS made a major contribution to revised BBC guidelines on reporting statistics (BBC 2017), while the BBC is also investing in data journalism – other broadcasters might follow their example.

- Establishing close links between statisticians and journalists, although this is not without problems (McConway 2016), and journalism training, such as is carried out by the RSS.
- Working with dedicated organisations, such as the Science Media Centre (2017) and Sense about Science (2017).
- Encouraging good story-telling with data, with appropriate and attractive narratives and visualisation.

Although there are many exhortations to turn numbers into stories, the process does carry risks. Stories need an arc and a well-rounded conclusion, which science rarely provides, and so it is tempting to over-simplify and over-claim. We need to encourage stories that are true to the evidence: its strengths, weaknesses, and uncertainties. We need, e.g., to be able to say that a drug or another medical intervention is neither good nor bad, that it has benefits and harms, that people might weigh them up in different ways and quite reasonably come to different conclusions. Journalists seem to shy away from such nuanced narratives, but, say, by including testimony from people with differing views, a good communicator should be able to make these stories gripping.

As an apparently rare example of such a story, Christie Ashwanden from FiveThirtyEight discussed the statistics about breast screening and then said that she had decided to avoid the procedure, whereas her smart friend, provided with the same evidence, had made the opposite decision (Aschwanden 2015). This neatly asserts the importance of personal values and concerns while still respecting the statistical evidence.

But it's not enough simply to invent lists of things that could be done to improve communication – we need active research into how best to do them. For example, how can we best communicate uncertainty about facts and the future without jeopardising trust and credibility, and how can our techniques be tailored to audiences with different attitudes and knowledge? In addition, there seems a remarkable lack of research into different ways of communicating how policy decisions are expected to impact society.

Trust as feeling and trust as analysis

The concept of a 'dual-process' in psychology has been popularised by Kahneman's image of thinking fast or slow: a rapid automatic non-conscious System 1 and a more considered conscious System 2 (Kahneman 2011). This idea has proved useful in examining different attitudes to risk: Slovic distinguishes 'risk as feelings', our immediate personal reactions to perceived threats, from 'risk as analysis', the analytic approach more familiar to statisticians and actuaries (Slovic et al. 2004).

Trust might be approached similarly. When we are the recipient of a claim, trust is generally viewed as a 'feeling', a product as much of whether we warm to the 'expert' as careful consideration of what is said: we've seen how pharma scientists suffer mistrust through broad suspicion of the industry. This is often a good heuristic, but like all heuristics it can be gamed by manipulative persuaders. In the spirit of Kahneman, we might distinguish 'fast trust' and 'slow trust', with fast trust dominated by our feelings about the topic and whether we feel the source shares our values and has our interests at heart. Slow trust is based on the type of considered inquiry and analysis encouraged by O'Neill.

But is it possible to move people from 'trust as feeling' to 'trust as analysis'? Can people be 'reasoned' out of gut feelings when they have an emotional investment in an opinion, and their 'motivated reasoning' means they are not shifted by evidence? This is not a new debate: in 1682 the English poet John Dryden optimistically claimed, *'A Man is to be cheated into Passion, but to be reason'd into Truth'* (Dryden 1682), but in 1721 Jonathan Swift presented a directly opposing view: *'Reasoning will never make a Man correct an ill Opinion, which by Reasoning he never acquired'* (Swift 1843).

An active area of research focusses on whether people's demonstrably inaccurate opinions can be corrected through provision of evidence. There are many studies of the 'backfire' effect, a form of confirmation bias, which says that simply correcting 'fake news' can end up reinforcing the very belief that is being countered. However, there is increasing evidence that misconceptions can to some extent be overcome by persuasive information (Spinney 2017), and studies show that it is possible to pre-emptively protect ('inoculate') public attitudes about climate change against real-world misinformation (Cook, Lewandowsky & Ecker 2017; van der Linden et al. 2017) and that good visualisations can improve 'immunity to misleading anecdote' (Fagerlin, Wang & Ubel 2005). People don't like to be deceived.

Improving the assessment of trustworthiness

There appear to be two main ways of ensuring that trustworthiness can be properly assessed: training audiences in critical appraisal and

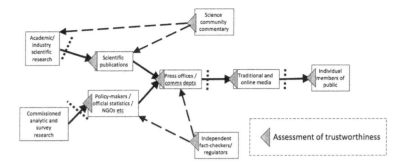

Figure 1.3 Potential for the assessment of trustworthiness of statistical evidence.

encouraging platforms dedicated to response and 'calling-out'. Possible routes are shown in Figure 1.3.

While each of the groups of 'assessors' will have different capacities and interests, rather similar principles should apply to whoever is considering the trustworthiness of statistical evidence, whether it is policy professionals critiquing the impact assessments provided by their analysts or patients confronted by information leaflets. For example, Stempra's *Guide to Being a Press Officer* emphasises the need to be clear about the limitations of the study (stempra 2017); Sense about Science have aimed directly at the public with their *Ask for Evidence* campaign (Sense about Science 2017); and recent randomised trials in Africa have shown that families can be taught, using comic books and audio lessons, to question claims made about medical treatments (Informed Health Choices 2017).

Training can involve the development of teaching and assessment material in critical appraisal; provision of check-lists; and awareness of tricks illustrated with gripping examples that are relevant to the specific audience. I've already mentioned Facebook and Full Fact's check-list for detecting 'false news', and I am pleased that the RSS is active in creating a more general list of questions that can be adapted to specific circumstances. Three aspects of a story can be critiqued:

- Questions about the *research* – i.e., the trustworthiness of the number itself ('internal validity').
- Questions about the *interpretation* – i.e., the trustworthiness of the conclusions drawn (external validity).
- Questions about the *communication* – i.e., the trustworthiness of the source and what we are being told (spin).

Figure 1.3 shows that fact-checkers, blogs, and official watchdogs, such as the UK Statistics Authority, can all publicly name-and-shame bad practice in the use of statistics. In contrast, the corresponding opportunity for the scientific community to comment on publications is mainly limited to a myriad of personal blogs due to the rather dysfunctional publication model that does not encourage even a moderated online discussion forum, even though the RSS has had published commentaries on papers for nearly two centuries. Short of retraction, there still seem to be few penalties for scientists indulging in questionable practices or slipping into advocacy.

The first step in good communication is to shut up and listen, and the flow of trustworthy evidence will only improve when providers are aware that at least part of their audience is carefully monitoring the quality of what is delivered and will publicly call them out if they deviate too much from competence, honesty, and reliability.

Conclusions

I have tried to bring together two related issues – lack of scientific reproducibility and dubious numbers in the news – by framing them as threats to trust, which should be countered by improving trustworthiness. The pipeline through which we receive information, complete with a series of filters, applies to both contexts, and the possible measures to improve trustworthiness of what is published in both the scientific and general media have much in common. Audiences need to be able to assess trustworthiness, and again the measures to improve their ability to do so are similar in both scientific and general media.

These are complex issues with many actors, of which the RSS is just one player, and we are fortunate that the UK has an active and collaborative ecology of organisations who are trying to improve the reliability of our science publications and the 'factfulness' of the media. Again, the RSS strapline, *Data, Evidence, Decisions*, has never been so pertinent, and it's a noble role to negotiate the delicate steps along that process. My personal heuristic is that statisticians are a trustworthy bunch, good and conscientious at their job, if a little nerdy. I believe they should have a higher profile in promoting impartial evidence, and this means that at least some need to become better at converting their insights into accessible (and trustworthy) stories.

Of course this endeavour is not restricted to those who would label themselves professional statisticians and join the RSS. Hans Rosling, master statistical story-teller, was a public health physician, and there is a growing and vibrant community of people who analyze and communicate data. Those who use, and misuse, statistics come from a wide variety of backgrounds, and so the aim must be to promote the trustworthiness of statistically based claims and decisions, not just the trustworthiness of statisticians. Nevertheless, when making such an assessment it may be reasonable to take into account the professionalism of the source.

I hope that the RSS will continue to be at the forefront of both improving the trustworthiness of the numbers used in society and the ability of audiences to assess that trustworthiness.

Acknowledgements

I am indebted to many for comments and encouragement on this diatribe, in particular Kevin McConway, Alex Freeman, Michael Blastland, Theresa Marteau, and Iain Wilton. And I could not be working in this area at all without the unquestioning support of David Harding of Winton Capital Management.

Notes

1 President's Address to the Royal Statistical Society.
2 We're all familiar with misunderstandings from using 'significance' as a technical term, but I had always thought of 'expected' as fairly innocuous. That was until a journalist labelled all hospital deaths above the expected level as 'unexpected'.
3 A letter on this topic was published in the Times during the current election campaign, with 114 signatories (including Baroness Onora O'Neill), reflecting the 114 people with pre-release access to labour market statistics.

References

Agnoli, F, Wicherts, JM, Veldkamp, CLS, Albiero, P & Cubelli, R 2017, 'Questionable research practices among Italian research psychologists', *PLOS ONE*, vol. 12, no. 3, e0172792. doi:10.1371/journal.pone.0172792.

Aschwanden, C 2015, October 20, Science won't settle the mammogram debate. Available from: https://fivethirtyeight.com/features/science-wont-settle-the-mammogram-debate/. [17 May 2017].

BBC 2017, Reporting statistics. Available from: http://downloads.bbc.co.uk/rmhttp/guidelines/editorialguidelines/pdfs/ReportingStatistics.pdf. [17 May 2017].

Begley, CG & Ioannidis, JPA 2015, 'Reproducibility in science: improving the standard for basic and preclinical research', *Circulation Research*, vol. 116, no. 1, pp. 116–126. doi:10.1161/CIRCRESAHA.114.303819.

Cook, J, Lewandowsky, S & Ecker, UKH 2017, Neutralizing misinformation through inoculation: exposing misleading argumentation techniques reduces their influence. *PLOS ONE*, vol. 12, no. 5, e0175799. doi:10.1371/journal.pone.0175799.

Cuddy, A 2012, *Your body language shapes who you are.* Available from: www.ted.com/talks/amy_cuddy_your_body_language_shapes_who_you_are.

Devlin, K 2009, February 15, Nine in 10 people carry gene which increases chance of high blood pressure. Available from: www.telegraph.co.uk/news/health/news/4630664/Nine-in-10-people-carry-gene-which-increases-chance-of-high-blood-pressure.html. [16 May 2017].

Donnelly, L 2016, Why binge watching your TV box-sets could kill you. Available from: www.telegraph.co.uk/news/2016/07/25/netflix-and-chill-could-lead-to-fatal-blood-clots-study-suggests/ [16 May 2017].

Dryden, J 1682, *Religio laici, or, A laymans faith a poem.* Available from: http://name.umdl.umich.edu/A36673.0001.001.

Edelman, 2017, Trust barometer. Available from: www.edelman.com/trust 2017/. [17 May 2017].

Fagerlin, A, Wang, C & Ubel, PA 2005, Reducing the influence of anecdotal reasoning on people's health care decisions: is a picture worth a thousand statistics? *Medical Decision Making: An International Journal of the Society for Medical Decision Making*, vol. 25, no. 4, pp. 398–405. doi:10.1177/0272989X05278931.

Fanelli, D 2009, 'How many scientists fabricate and falsify research? A systematic review and meta-analysis of survey data', *PLoS ONE*, vol. 4, no. 5, e5738. doi:10.1371/journal.pone.0005738.

Fox, F 2012, 10 best practice guidelines for reporting science & health stories. Available from: http://webarchive.nationalarchives.gov.uk/20140122145147/http://www.levesoninquiry.org.uk/wp-content/uploads/2012/07/Second-Submission-to-inquiry-Guidelines-for-Science-and-Health-Reporting.pdf. [18 May 2017].

Full Fact 2017, Full Fact is the UK's independent fact checking organisation. Available from: https://fullfact.org. [16 May 2017].

Gelman, A 2013, September 26, Difficulties in making inferences about scientific truth from distributions of published p-values. Available from: http://andrewgelman.com/2013/09/26/difficulties-in-making-inferences-about-scientific-truth-from-distributions-of-published-p-values/ [16 May 2017].

Gelman, A & Loken, E 2014, 'The statistical crisis in science', *American Scientist*, vol. 102, no. 6, p. 460. doi:10.1511/2014.111.460.

Gelman, A & Stern, H 2006, 'The difference between "significant" and "not significant" is not itself statistically significant', *The American Statistician*, vol. 60, no. 4, pp. 328–331. doi:10.1198/000313006X152649.

Gregory, A 2017, Why going to university increases risk of getting a brain tumour - Mirror Online. Available from: www.mirror.co.uk/science/going-university-increases-risk-getting-8239162. [16 May 2017].

Informed Health Choices 2017, Using evidence to change the world. Available from: www.informedhealthchoices.org/. [18 May 2017].

Ioannidis, J 2014, 'Discussion: why "An estimate of the science-wise false discovery rate and application to the top medical literature" is false', *Biostatistics*, vol. 15, no. 1, pp. 28–36. doi:10.1093/biostatistics/kxt036.

Ioannidis, JPA 2005, 'Why most published research findings are false', *PLoS Med*, vol. 2, no. 8, p. 8, e124. doi:10.1371/journal.pmed.0020124.

Jager, LR & Leek, JT 2014, 'An estimate of the science-wise false discovery rate and application to the top medical literature', *Biostatistics*, vol. 15, no. 1, pp. 1–12. doi:10.1093/biostatistics/kxt007.

John, LK, Loewenstein, G & Prelec D 2012, 'Measuring the prevalence of questionable research practices with incentives for truth telling', *Psychological Science*, vol. 23, no. 5, pp. 524–532. doi:10.1177/0956797611430953.

Kahneman, D 2011, *Thinking, Fast and Slow*, Farrar, Straus and Giroux, New York.

Khanolkar, AR, Ljung, R, Talbäck, M, Brooke, HL, Carlsson, S, Mathiesen, T & Feychting, M 2016, 'Socioeconomic position and the risk of brain tumour: a Swedish national population-based cohort study', *Journal of Epidemiology and Community Health*, vol. 70, no. 12, pp. 1222–1228. doi:10.1136/jech-2015-207002.

Leek, JT & Jager, LR 2017, 'Is most published research really false?' *Annual Review of Statistics and Its Application*, vol. 4, no. 1, pp. 109–122. doi:10.1146/annurev-statistics-060116-054104.

Makri, A 2017, 'Give the public the tools to trust scientists', *Nature News*, vol. 541, no. 7637, p. 261. doi:10.1038/541261a.

Matthews, R, Wasserstein, R & Spiegelhalter, D 2017, 'The ASA's *p* -value statement, one year on', *Significance*, vol. 14, no. 2, pp. 38–41. doi:10.1111/j.1740-9713.2017.01021.x.

McConway, K 2016, 'Statistics and the media: a statistician's view', *Journalism*, vol. 17, no. 1, 49–65. doi:10.1177/1464884915593243.

Medical Xpress 2016, High levels of education linked to heightened brain tumor risk. Available from: https://medicalxpress.com/news/2016-06-high-linked-heightened-brain-tumor.html. [16 May 2017].

Mervis, J 2017, March 24, Data check: NSF sends congress a garbled message on misconduct numbers. Available from: www.sciencemag.org/news/2017/03/data-check-nsf-sends-congress-garbled-message-misconduct-numbers. [16 May 2017].

Munafò, MR, Nosek, BA, Bishop, DVM, Button, KS, Chambers, CD, Percie du Sert, N, ... Ioannidis, JPA 2017, 'A manifesto for reproducible science', *Nature Human Behaviour*, vol. 1, no. 1, p. 0021. doi:10.1038/s41562-016-0021.

NATCEN Social Research 2017, Public confidence in official statistics. Available from: http://natcen.ac.uk/our-research/research/public-confidence-in-official-statistics/. [17 May 2017].

Newton-Cheh, C, Johnson, T, Gateva, V, Tobin, MD, Bochud, M, Coin, L, ... Munroe, PB 2009, 'Genome-wide association study identifies eight loci associated with blood pressure', *Nature Genetics*, vol. 41, no. 6, pp. 666–676. doi:10.1038/ng.361.

O'Neill, O 2002, *A question of trust: The BBC Reith lectures 2002*, Cambridge University Press, Cambridge.

O'Neill, O 2013, What we don't understand about trust. Available from: www. ted.com/talks/onora_o_neill_what_we_don_t_understand_about_trust/ transcript?language=en. [17 May 2017].

Open Science Collaboration 2015, 'Estimating the reproducibility of psychological science', *Science*, vol. 349, no. 6251, aac4716–aac4716. doi:10.1126/ science.aac4716.

Patil, P, Peng, RD & Leek, JT 2016, 'What should researchers expect when they replicate studies? A statistical view of replicability in psychological science', *Perspectives on Psychological Science*, vol. 11, no. 4, pp. 539–544. doi:10.1177/1745691616646366.

Ranehill, E, Dreber, A, Johannesson, M, Leiberg, S, Sul, S & Weber, RA 2015, 'Assessing the robustness of power posing: no effect on hormones and risk tolerance in a large sample of men and women', *Psychological Science*, vol. 26, no. 5, pp. 653–656. doi:10.1177/0956797614553946.

Royal Society 2012, Science as an open enterprise. Available from: https:// royalsociety.org/topics-policy/projects/science-public-enterprise/report/. [17 May 2017].

Royal Statistical Society 2016, Data manifesto. Available from: www.rss.org. uk/RSS/Influencing_Change/Data_manifesto/RSS/Influencing_Change/ Data_democracy_sub/Data_manifesto.aspx?hkey=5dd70207-82e7-4166-93fd-bcf9a2a1e496. [18 May 2017].

Science Media Centre 2017, Where science meets the headlines. Available from: www.sciencemediacentre.org/. [18 May 2017].

Sense about Science 2017, Because evidence matters. Available from: http:// senseaboutscience.org/. [18 May 2017].

Shafik, M 2017, In experts we trust? Available from: www.bankofengland. co.uk/publications/Documents/speeches/2017/speech964.pdf. [17 May 2017].

Shirakawa, T, Iso, H, Yamagishi, K, Yatsuya, H, Tanabe, N, Ikehara, S, ... Tamakoshi, A, 2016, 'Watching television and risk of mortality from pulmonary embolism among Japanese men and women: table.: the JACC study (Japan collaborative cohort)', *Circulation*, vol. 134, no. 4, pp. 355–357. doi:10.1161/CIRCULATIONAHA.116.023671.

Simmons, JP, Nelson, LD & Simonsohn, U 2011, 'False-positive psychology: undisclosed flexibility in data collection and analysis allows presenting anything as significant', *Psychological Science*, vol. 22, no. 11, pp. 1359–1366. doi:10.1177/0956797611417632.

Slovic, P, Finucane, ML, Peters, E & MacGregor, DG 2004, 'Risk as analysis and risk as feelings: some thoughts about affect, reason, risk, and rationality', *Risk Analysis*, vol. 24, no. 2, pp. 311–322. doi:10.1111/j.0272-4332.2004. 00433.x.

Spinney, L 2017, 'How Facebook, fake news and friends are warping your memory', *Nature News*, vol. 543, no. 7644, p. 168. doi:10.1038/543168a.

stempra. 2017, Guide to being a press officer. Available from: https://stempra. org.uk/wp-content/themes/stempra/downloads/2017_stempra_guide_to_ being_a_media_officer.pdf. [17 May 2017].

Sumner, P, Vivian-Griffiths, S, Boivin, J, Williams, A, Bott, L, Adams, R, Venetis CA, Whelan L, Hughes B, Chambers, CD 2016, 'Exaggerations and caveats in press releases and health-related science news', *PLOS ONE*, vol. 11, no. 12, e0168217. doi:10.1371/journal.pone.0168217.

Sumner, P, Vivian-Griffiths, S, Boivin, J, Williams, A, Venetis, CA, Davies, A, Ogden J, Whelan L, Hughes B, Dalton B, Boy F, Chambers, CD 2014, 'The association between exaggeration in health related science news and academic press releases: retrospective observational study', *BMJ*, vol. 349(dec09 7), g7015–g7015. doi:10.1136/bmj.g7015.

Swift, J, 1843, *The works of Jonathan swift ...: containing interesting and valuable papers, not hitherto published ... with memoir of the author.* Henry G. Bohn.

Szucs, D & Ioannidis, JPA 2017, Empirical assessment of published effect sizes and power in the recent cognitive neuroscience and psychology literature. *PLOS Biology, 15*(3), e2000797. doi:10.1371/journal.pbio.2000797.

Tetlock, PE & Gardner, D 2015, *Superforecasting: The art and science of prediction.* McClelland & Stewart.

van der Linden, S, Leiserowitz, A, Rosenthal, S & Maibach, E 2017, Inoculating the public against misinformation about climate change. *Global Challenges, 1*(2), 1600008. doi:10.1002/gch2.201600008.

Wasserstein, RL & Lazar, NA 2016, 'The ASA's statement on *p*-values: context, process, and purpose', *The American Statistician*, vol. 70, no. 2, pp. 129–133. doi:10.1080/00031305.2016.1154108.

Wellcome Trust, 2017, Public views on medical research. Available from: https://wellcome.ac.uk/what-we-do/our-work/public-views-medical-research. [17 May 2017].

YouGov 2017, Leave voters are less likely to trust any experts – even weather forecasters. Available from: //yougov.co.uk/news/2017/02/17/leave-voters-are-less-likely-trust-any-experts-eve/. [17 May 2017].

YouTube 2016, Gove: Britons "Have Had Enough of Experts." Available from: www.youtube.com/watch?v=GGgiGtJk7MA. [17 May 2017].

2 Science policy in a post-truth world

Emma Woods

From where I stand

On December 12, 2015, exhausted after a long stint at the United Nations (UN) climate talks in Paris, the news reached me: for the first time, world leaders had reached agreement on the need to tackle climate change. The Paris Agreement was a victory on many fronts, not least for science as it sent a clear signal that politicians had listened to the overwhelming scientific consensus. Fast forward to June 1, 2017 and the victory had turned sour. Following claims by US President Donald Trump that climate change was a "hoax", the USA – the world's biggest emitter of greenhouse gases per capita – was pulling out of the deal. This was the post-truth phenomenon writ large and a wake-up call for proponents of science and evidence.

The post-truth phenomenon affects different people in different ways. For some it's a threat, for others it's an opportunity, and for others it's a curiosity. My own encounter comes from the perspective of "science policy" or "evidence-based policy".

As Head of Policy at the Royal Society, the UK's national academy of science, I work with some of the world's most distinguished scientists to provide expert, timely, and independent advice to policymakers – on topics from fracking to genetically modified (GM) crops, extreme weather to nature conservation. Above all, my role involves navigating diverse worlds and worldviews, brokering knowledge and relationships, and translating evidence into usable knowledge that benefits decision-makers and society at large. By decision-makers I mean not only the UK government but also the UN, regulatory bodies, businesses, and other influencers. And as well as influencing specific policy decisions, my aim is to inform public life and debate more widely.

While not a subject expert in risk, trust, or uncertainty, the demands of science policy mean that I am drawn into these areas almost by default. The post-truth phenomenon simply adds to the adventure by introducing new or newly guised challenges that need navigating as well as new opportunities for those with the skills to seize them.

Here I look at what a post-truth world might mean for science policy. Then, drawing on my own experience, I propose two ways of upgrading science policy for that new world. The first is through evidence synthesis. This means ensuring that trustworthy synthesised evidence is readily available across all areas of science and policy – much as it was for leaders negotiating the Paris Agreement, in the form of authoritative reports by the Intergovernmental Panel on Climate Change. The second is through public dialogue. This means engaging the public in ways that reveal new articulations of the questions we should be asking and that boost the legitimacy of public policy – again, not unlike the broad engagement that surrounded the Paris talks and helped steer them towards the final deal. Ultimately I reflect on the fact that the addition of a post-truth filter to an already-complex science policy landscape might be no bad thing. It might encourage greater scrutiny and rigour, and might lead us to consider new and improved modes of evidence-based policymaking that are more inclusive and transparent.

The trials and tribulations of science policy

Many accounts of science policy will begin by acknowledging the distinct worlds of science and policy. These are worlds with different values, constraints, and approaches to risk and uncertainty, as well as different levels of trust afforded to them by the public. These differences and the challenge of bridging the gaps between them are well-documented (Doubleday and Wilsdon 2013). So too are suggestions for how to inch these worlds towards each other, with helpful guides such as "Top 20 things scientists need to know about policy-making" (Tyler 2013) and "Top 20 things politicians need to know about science" (Milman 2013).

My own experience of navigating within and between these distinct worlds has taught me several things. Perhaps most fundamental is the fact that scientists and policymakers have very different relationships with evidence – what it is, how relevant it is, and how complete it needs to be. To give a crude characterisation: an academic scientist who may have invested considerable amounts of time, money, and effort in her research may consider the resulting evidence to be the most important thing a policymaker needs to know. By contrast, a policymaker weighing up a range of policy options is likely to consider those options through multiple lenses, of which the evidence is merely one.

Other lenses might include the personal and political values held by different people, the policy objectives (which may themselves be contested), and the extent to which an "ideal" solution can actually be delivered on the ground (Peplow 2014). In such complex and contested situations, evidence is necessary but not sufficient.

Even where evidence is considered essential to the task at hand, time pressures, competing policy priorities, and limited skills and networks on the part of policymakers can contribute to evidence being overlooked. In addition, a lack of communication and understanding between the policy and research communities can create an unintended disconnect between the questions policymakers are grappling with and the availability of evidence that has the potential to provide insight.

Added to this challenge is the fact that scientists and policymakers often hold differing views on the importance of *complete* evidence. This can result in good evidence not being available within policy-relevant timeframes. A typical scientist will often prefer to take her time to boost the rigour and completeness of her research, thereby reducing biases and uncertainties. However, in public policy it may be that a good enough answer before a decision is taken is considerably more valuable than a perfect one that arrives a day too late (provided the limitations imposed by doing it quickly are made clear) (Whitty 2015).

There can also be a fine line to tread between accuracy and usefulness. On the one hand, evidence should convey sufficient uncertainty so as to accurately describe reality and meet the requirements of the scientific community. On the other hand, it should be sufficiently clear and conclusive so as to actually be useful to policymakers. The scientist who, invited to give evidence to a Minister, uses her time to say *"the science is all very complex and uncertain"* is unlikely to be invited back. Indeed, it is often said in science policy that a statement of evidence can never be fully accurate *and* useful (Stilgoe 2013).

Just to make the balancing act even more challenging, there are worldviews and communities besides just "science" and "policy" to consider. Marshalling evidence to inform policy often involves bringing together communities that exist as siloes in science and/or policy – convening the public health community and the environmental community, say, to discuss air quality. Doing this allows trends, challenges, and solutions to be explored in a more holistic way that reflects the complex reality of a situation rather than the simplistic structures of government or university departments. In working across a whole range of interdisciplinary policy issues – from building resilience to extreme weather to considering the future of human genome editing – I've come to accept the "joined up" jargon as an inevitable and necessary mainstay.

How the post-truth phenomenon ups the ante

The craft of science policy – navigating diverse worlds, brokering knowledge and relationships, and translating evidence into usable knowledge about what we know and don't know – is challenging at the best of times. But while many of the challenges are predictable, enduring, and recurrent, some – such as the post-truth phenomenon – are evolving.

Post-truth is defined by Oxford Dictionaries as "relating to or denoting circumstances in which objective facts are less influential in shaping public opinion than appeals to emotion and personal belief". It doesn't equate to simply not telling the truth, but rather to a situation in which some types of truth are of secondary importance.

Post-truth is not a new phenomenon (in fact the term was first used by Tesich in 1992), but instead a continuation of previous trends in politics and in some senses a rebranding. Politics has arguably always been more about values than facts, and, as mentioned, evidence is only one lens through which policy options are viewed. Post-truth is also not new to science. Debates around climate change, alternative medicine, and vaccination have arguably been in post-truth territory for years.

However, the post-truth phenomenon is receiving more attention at present because it has encroached into the heart of policymaking rather than being confined to narrower or more peripheral issues. The explosion of post-truth commentaries on processes such as the Brexit vote and US presidency campaign illustrates this point. In this context it is perhaps unsurprising that post-truth was named 2016 "word of the year" by Oxford Dictionaries.

Changing interactions between people and information

One of the most salient ways in which post-truth intensifies the task of science policy is that it shifts how people and information interact. Even before we recognised the post-truth phenomenon, the volume of information in the world was increasing. Every year there are over two million new academic publications (Scopus 2018), and this new information hasn't necessarily come with increased comprehensibility or a handy guide for how to make best use of it.

Against this background of academic publishing are new forms of online noise. While the internet has in many ways changed people's interaction with information for the better – democratising knowledge and allowing a more diverse range of inputs which arguably foster "the wisdom of crowds" (Surowiecki 2005) – it has also brought a cacophony of misinformation. This includes so-called "fake news" or "alternative facts", which are either deliberately false stories or stories that have some truth but are biased or use unreliable sources (Baker 2017). Anyone can publish in the unregulated worlds of Twitter and Facebook, and we are seeing an increase in "clickbait" – sensationalist stories designed to encourage web traffic onto a site of sometimes dubious truthfulness. This online environment can mean that false information circulates and gains traction rapidly, and that unusual or exceptional cases receive unwarranted attention.

Other exacerbating factors are the "filter bubbles" created by computer algorithms, machine learning, and the digital news environment, which can mean that users are exposed to more tailored news, to like-minded people, and ultimately to a narrower version of the world. This can lead to "echo chambers" in which fringe beliefs become more established and persistent, perspectives become polarised, and people's awareness of views that differ from their own diminishes.

All this contributes to the risk that public debate and policy decisions are based on concerns from the electorate inspired by misrepresented or overhyped information. In this context, it is increasingly important that policy and debate are informed by the current best evidence and that, where possible, this evidence is available to all, in formats and media where it will be consumed.

Changing trust in institutions and expertise

The post-truth phenomenon is often associated with eroding trust in science and expertise, and a rejection or suspicion of institutions that are grounded in evidence-based policies (from government to the media to the law). Under this reading of post-truth, both science and policy are at stake. Interestingly, concerns about expertise seem less about the validity of academic methods and more about the motivations of some experts, who can be perceived as presenting facts selectively, confusing the public with complexity, and conflating values and evidence.

Mixed in with this alleged distrust, is the increasing realisation that "non-expert" voices should not be marginalised or ignored and that the legitimacy of policymaking relies on broad and genuine engagement (Chwalisz 2017). Many have argued that the recent assaults on elites in Europe and the USA have been driven in part by the feeling that the views of the populace have been structurally excluded from the levers of power (Noveck 2015).

There can be a tendency to rail against the negative aspects of a post-truth world – and indeed, there are very real threats to the work I do. The Royal Society has a long-standing reputation as an independent, impartial, and trusted broker of knowledge to inform public life. If science really is losing (or perceived to be losing) its standing as a trustworthy source of truth, then it becomes even more important for institutions like the Royal Society to engage, adapt, and respond.

However, there are positives to be found in a post-truth world too. In many ways the shifts in how we interact with information and expertise are simply expressions of how knowledge, including scientific knowledge, is becoming democratised, and how diverse articulations of problems are being expressed.

Whether good or bad, today's unique brand of post-truth needs recognising and adjusting to. It presents risks and opportunities, and those with the skills to target, marshal, and deploy evidence most inclusively and most effectively will be at a premium. So, how to most successfully navigate this new landscape to ensure well-founded public policy and debate?

A role for evidence synthesis

My first tip for successful navigation is evidence synthesis – in other words, moving to a world in which high quality synthesised evidence is readily available across all areas of science and policy.

Evidence synthesis refers to the process of bringing together a large amount of information from a range of sources and disciplines and turning it into accessible, usable knowledge to inform debates and decisions. Synthesis comes in many shapes and sizes: from a formal systematic review over months or years (such as the Cochrane Reviews common in medicine) to the rapid drawing together of evidence to inform an emergency situation (as was the case following the 2011 Fukushima earthquake and nuclear disaster).

Policymakers will typically ask *"What's the evidence for that?"* What they tend to mean (although rarely phrase it as such) is *"Has sufficient synthesis of all the evidence been done in relation to that?"* Policy questions are rarely (if ever) answered by a single study or even by a single discipline. Decision-making and public debate are best served if policymakers have access to *all* the relevant evidence relating to a particular issue. This involves an important step – evidence synthesis – between research being conducted and decisions being taken. Indeed, an accurate, concise, and unbiased synthesis of the evidence is arguably one of the most valuable contributions the research community can offer policymakers (Whitty 2015).

Synthesis is perhaps even more important in a post-truth world. It has the potential to cut through the noisy and confusing information landscape and to reduce the risk of misinformation taking hold. In the context of heightened scrutiny of experts and the foundations on which decisions are made, synthesis also presents information transparently and helpfully recasts the role of the expert. The expert is no longer a source of specific knowledge but rather someone who is able to curate and present the consensus in a scientific or political field.

Principles for good evidence synthesis for policy

I recently led a process to agree a set of principles for good evidence synthesis for policy (Figure 2.1). These were developed by the Royal Society and Academy of Medical Sciences (2018) and have been subsequently endorsed by UK Research and Innovation, the Government Office for Science, the Department for Environment, Food and Rural Affairs, the Department of Health and Social Care, the Civil Service Policy Profession, (with the exception of committing to free access to all syntheses) *Nature* (Donnelly et al. 2018).

The principles outline the fundamental features that should apply to any evidence synthesis regardless of the timeframe, topic, or method. They are intended to promote the spread of synthesis by making it easier for policymakers, researchers, and knowledge brokers to identify, use, conduct, and commission good synthesis. Ultimately, if the principles are followed they should provide assurances that the resulting

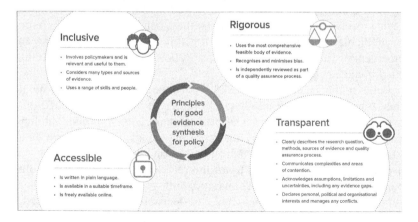

Figure 2.1 Principles for good evidence synthesis for policy.
Note: Image adapted from the Royal Society and the Academy of Medical Sciences.

synthesised evidence is trustworthy (competent, honest, and reliable (O'Neill 2013)) – and in doing so support well-founded policymaking and public debate in a post-truth world.

Inclusive synthesis

Inclusive evidence synthesis that involves policymakers throughout – from designing the research question to interpreting the findings – is most likely to yield important policy insights. Keeping the process inclusive makes it more likely to identify the full range of relevant evidence types and sources. Depending on the focus and purpose of the synthesis, relevant evidence might include published and unpublished academic literature, research conducted in industry or by NGOs, policy evaluation studies from different countries and contexts, and expert and public opinion.

UK Government Foresight projects are a good example of inclusive synthesis. On topics from flooding to mental capacity, obesity to global food and farming, they typically take 12 months or so and involve around 200 researchers from the full range of sciences through to the arts and humanities. As well as ensuring that all relevant evidence is considered, an inclusive process helps avoid the all-too-common situation in which experts are used inexpertly (Sutherland and Burgman 2015) and "group think" and narrow echo chambers of expertise come to dominate.

Rigorous synthesis

Rigorous synthesis should consider the most comprehensive body of evidence and should minimise bias at every stage of the process. This is bias in the sense of anything that distorts the evidence or analysis in a misleading manner, as well as personal prejudice which has no place whatsoever in good synthesis. In this way, synthesis continues the tradition of a quarter of a century of evidence-based medicine – which itself emerged in response to the need for more critical evaluation of facts in medical practice. For many, Cochrane, a global network of researchers, professionals, carers, and people interested in health, continues to set the standard for rigorous synthesis to inform healthcare decisions.

Good practice now extends well beyond medicine. The Campbell Collaboration provides a similar service for decision-making in education, social welfare, crime and justice, and international development. In both cases, co-ordinating groups minimise bias through pre-defined methodologies, training for authors, rigorous quality assurance processes, and a significant amount of time (typically two years or so) to undertake the synthesis. Similarly, the Intergovernmental Panel on Climate Change ensures rigour through the sheer number of participants (thousands of authors and reviewers) and time taken (around five years) to craft an Assessment Report.

Transparent synthesis

Evidence synthesis that is transparent is more likely to be credible, replicable, and useful in its own right, and as a basis for undertaking further synthesis. The description of a study's design should include the search terms used, the databases and other evidence sources considered and when they were accessed, and the criteria that determined which sources were and weren't included and why. Studies should also explicitly acknowledge complexities and areas of strong consensus and contention – particularly where there are fundamental disagreements within the project team – in order to help policymakers interpret the findings and to inform evidence-based public debate more widely.

Oxford Martin Restatements, which review the scientific evidence on policy issues from bovine tuberculosis to ionising radiation, provide a powerful example of this by explicitly grading the quality of the evidence and classifying each paragraph using a set of descriptive codes. For instance, the *[Projn]* code means "projection based on available evidence but with substantial uncertainties". The Intergovernmental Panel on Climate Change is also widely lauded for its clear assessments of the strength of evidence (qualified as "limited", "medium", or "robust") and the degree of agreement among authors ("low", "medium", or "high"). Returning to my earlier point about the tension between being accurate and useful, uncertainties need to be clearly communicated without providing so many layers of caveat upon caveat that the overriding messages become obscured.

Transparency is arguably even more important in a post-truth world. The lack of reliable methods for communicating uncertainty about the conclusions we draw from data is often blamed for the sharpening distrust of experts. Even the most rigorous scientific methods do not lead us to certainty; yet the media and public commentators so often present (or encourage researchers to present) uncertain conclusions as certainties. When such conclusions fail to be 100 per cent accurate, as is inevitable with uncertain conclusions, the public trust in, and credibility of, experts is damaged.

Some have suggested that transparency in the presentation of evidence could be taken one step further – going beyond just "showing your working" to transparently pre-empting the sorts of methods that might spread misinformation or contradict the evidence being presented. In this way, evidence providers might be able to "inoculate" the public against misinformation by providing information about the methods used to obscure or deny facts alongside the facts themselves (van der Linden et al. 2017).

Accessible synthesis

For synthesised evidence to be both useful and used it must be accessible. It should be written in plain language by a writer who is experienced in presenting information clearly and concisely, and as objectively as possible. A good example of this is the Royal Society's 2017 report on machine learning, which includes two types of summary – one for policymakers and one for the wider public, with the latter both printed and associated with online infographics to demonstrate machine learning in practice.

Synthesised evidence should also be made available in time to contribute to the decision-making process. And in all but the most confidential situations, the full text and search terms should be published in an open access repository to allow the synthesis to be extended, reproduced, or updated in light of new evidence.

As mentioned, evidence will never be the only factor being considered by policymakers, and synthesised evidence will be quickly discarded if it is inaccessible – whether full of technical jargon, hidden behind a journal paywall, or made available too late. In the context of fake news and alternative facts, it is increasingly important that high quality synthesised evidence is readily available to all.

Changes to the research and policy landscapes

The principles indicate what good synthesis looks like. But this is only the first step. We need to create a more effective marketplace for synthesis: one in which policymakers and commentators reach out to where accessible and timely evidence is available, and one in which academics are engaged in synthesising evidence because they know it will make a difference.

To ensure that high quality synthesis is more widely used to inform policy and practice, the research and policy landscapes will need to evolve, and cultures will need to change. Universities, funders, and publishers need to create the incentives, rewards, and research culture that support evidence synthesis and give it the status it deserves – as a means of getting better value from primary research and as an intellectually stimulating and respected research endeavour in its own right. Government can help too by proactively communicating its evidence needs, working with researchers to co-produce syntheses, and consistently citing the evidence that has informed policy decisions.

Central to these cultural shifts are the ideas of collaboration, co-production, and brokerage – the starting point for the science policy mission (Owens 2015). University bodies (such as the Cambridge Centre for Science and Policy), non-governmental organisations, and the policy divisions of learned societies (like the Royal Society) can help create this sort of enabling environment. By brokering conversations and longer-lasting relationships between academics and policymakers, they can make it easier for researchers to appreciate the sorts of issues policymakers are dealing with and for policymakers to seek out the evidence they need.

A role for public dialogue

A core feature of evidence synthesis is the inclusion of diverse types and sources of evidence. Depending on the aim of the synthesis, the relative importance of these types and sources will vary. If the aim is to demonstrate causality (say, the effect of a particular drug on a disease), then only high quality quantitative academic research may be relevant. If the aim is to inform more complex societal debates (say, how to tackle childhood obesity), then qualitative evidence, anecdotal evidence, and public opinion may come into play.

In a post-truth world public opinion is not only being expressed in new ways online but is also increasingly being recognised as an important contribution to more inclusive and legitimate policymaking. When it comes to science policy in particular, science can tell us what is possible. But in a democracy everyone in society needs to be involved in the discussion about what should be done, why, and for what purposes.

This is not to downplay the importance of purely technical evidence, but rather to say that it can only take us so far. Diversity and plurality are key. Multiple perspectives from industry, the law, the media, special interest groups, and other publics should be invited into the conversation. Doing this means that approaches that are taken for granted in particular circles – such as those that originate from scientists and their research agendas – can be critiqued and recalibrated in light of alternative perspectives (Jasanoff and Hurlbut 2018). This view aligns with long-expressed calls for a new "social contract for science";

one which ensures that scientific knowledge is "socially robust" and that its production is seen by society to be both transparent and participatory (Gibbons 1999).

The case of genetic technologies

My own career has touched on several forms of participatory research and dialogue, predominantly in the UK and East Africa. I began by conducting my own research on Participatory Video as a method for both elucidating people's views about nature and bringing marginalised voices to the eyes and ears of decision-makers. I subsequently worked to implement community-based natural resource management schemes informed by local and indigenous knowledge.

My most recent encounter comes from the Royal Society's work on genetic technologies. Scientific developments are making it faster, easier, and cheaper to understand, make, and adapt genetic material, with the result that some previously theoretical uses of genetic technologies are becoming increasingly possible. But as well as considering what now can be done, scientists and society must also consider what *should* be done.

To contribute to the wider debates that are necessary, in 2017 the Royal Society commissioned a public dialogue in the UK to explore the range of views that people hold about which applications of genetic technologies should be developed, why, and under what conditions. This involved a deliberative process which put a representative sample of the UK population in front of scientists and ethicists who acted as honest and neutral knowledge brokers. Through a range of activities, over several weeks and in three UK locations (London, Edinburgh, and Norwich), approximately 90 participants were given the opportunity to ask questions, to offer their own views, and to develop their thinking through a process of reflection and re-evaluation (Hopkins Van Mil 2018).

In what follows I examine how well-designed public dialogue can provide valuable insights into the different ways that challenges are articulated and risks perceived, into the frames and contexts that moderate public acceptability, and into the ways in which opinions evolve throughout the deliberative process. In a post-truth world, such insights give us not only a richer body of evidence to inform policy, but also an understanding of the sorts of policy questions we should be asking in the first place. Public dialogue can therefore be a concrete step towards more legitimate and socially intelligent policymaking that resonates with the public and earns their confidence.

Articulating challenges and updating the narrative

Public dialogue reveals the different ways that the public articulates challenges. In the context of science policy, this is hugely important to know. Scientific evidence will only ever be one factor informing a policy decision, and its relevance can be diminished if it is seen to come from a skewed (often "techno-optimistic") standpoint. If scientists alone are left to identify and articulate the most pressing challenges they are more likely to start with the science or technology itself rather than with the societal trend towards which the science (among a whole range of other things) might contribute. Evidence-based policy relies not only on good evidence but also on the right questions being asked. For this reason, horizon scanning by scientists or scientific institutions is often criticised, as is public engagement that starts with the technological solution rather than the societal challenge.

In the context of post-truth, where people can feel excluded from policy decisions or can feel that debates are being had on issues or in ways that they can't relate to, the appreciation and inclusion of public articulations of challenges can help make policymaking more inclusive and legitimate.

The genetic technologies public dialogue revealed how the narrative around these technologies might be reframed to encourage more fruitful public and political debate. This involves moving from a simplistic framing of "for" or "against" the technologies in general to a more nuanced framing that considers specific uses for specific purposes (say, using genome editing to make drought-tolerant wheat) in the context of a range of options for dealing with major societal challenges (say, the challenge of increasing instances of drought under climate change).

The public dialogue elaborated on this point by revealing the particular frames and contexts that moderate people's support for genetic technologies. It revealed that people care about things like equitable access to technologies, collective welfare, positive environmental outcomes, and transparency. In turn, they find unacceptable any uses of genetic technologies that erode diversity, prioritise individual or corporate wealth, and restrict freedom of choice (Hopkins Van Mil 2018).

This finding is consistent with much of the literature about science in society, which reminds us that technology is not good or bad in and of itself and that publics are far more concerned with how it is used, why, for what purpose, and for whose benefit (Pidgeon and Henwood 2014). Many disputes about GM crops have been, in part, concerns about multinational companies and their motivations. About 15 years ago when GM was just emerging, its main proponents and many of the initial products were from large multinationals (even though it was publicly funded scientists who produced much of the initial research). Understandably, many felt GM was a means for these corporations to maximise their profits and objected on that basis (Ramakrishnan 2017).

People, like policymakers, look at issues through several different lenses, and it is important to debate each on its own terms. Concerns about genetic technologies might relate to globalisation and multinational corporations, or might relate to the safety of a particular technique. Both are entirely legitimate concerns, but it can be counterproductive to debate one when the concern is really the other. Without diverse public expressions of concern, those at the forefront of research can all too readily revert to the question of physical safety and in doing so can short-circuit the debate, exclude important perspectives, and entrench a post-truth suspicion of experts.

Learning curves

Structured public dialogue also helps us to understand how people interact with, reflect on, and learn from evidence – an important consideration for science policy, let alone science policy in a post-truth world.

The deliberative model of dialogue with time for reflection and re-evaluation that was used in the genetic technologies case led to participants moving along several learning curves: from knowing nothing or very little to feeling they would be more aware of and interested in the topic in future; from generalised fear to cautious optimism and preferences for particular uses of the technology over others; and from thinking the dialogue was another tick box exercise to thinking that voices had genuinely been listened to and would inform future work.

The process also led many participants to revise their perceptions of risk. Many increasingly realised that while all change brings risk, not changing brings risk too. Much discussed initially were potentially catastrophic risks resulting from intended or unintended action – that we will release diseases dangerous to humans, plants, or animals, or that a biological weapon could be produced. Harder to visualise, at least at first, were risks associated with gradual change – that through our choices now we might inadvertently arrive at a future state we didn't want and haven't consented to.

A few participants' reflections on the deliberative process included (Hopkins Van Mil 2018):

- It was really informative and has given me an opportunity to listen to people who are really experts in the field, listen to their insights as well as their knowledge, as well as talking to peers about our fears, concerns and hopes for a future with genetic technologies. The process has been, for me, very positive.

(London)

• I think the process is very important. I think for the scientists and wider legislative bodies one of the most important things you can do is engage with society and find out what they really want. I think there is a lot of scope and more institutions should be doing similar things.

(Edinburgh)

• In the first session we had to deal with huge issues but having that space to talk with my friends, to think about it and to do my own research was incredibly valuable because now, today, I've got a lot more out of it. I have learnt from it.

(Norwich)

This sort of structured dialogue highlights the fact that when people vote they don't generally have the opportunity to engage in technical discussions – but that if they did, they might think differently about the issues. In this way, dialogue can go some way to addressing the post-truth challenges of people not having access to sufficiently trustworthy information and people feeling excluded from decision-making processes.

Cause for hope?

The post-truth phenomenon is often portrayed as a bad thing. Indeed, I've explored here how it challenges the expertise represented by science, policy, and their respective institutions, and how it therefore adds an extra layer of complexity to an already-challenging science policy landscape.

However, with the arrival of post-truth has come greater scrutiny – generally focussing on the motivations of some experts who can be perceived as presenting facts selectively, confusing the public with complexity and conflating values and evidence. To me these seem entirely valid things to scrutinise.

From a historical perspective, scrutinising experts has played an important role in public life and the advancement of knowledge. Although today we hold the 18th century Enlightenment responsible for both good and bad things, its central tenets of promoting rational inquiry, critical thinking, and scientific achievement and literacy must surely be applauded (Pagden 2013). Central to this mission was the idea of challenging established modes of practice and traditional authority, along with a commitment to engaging with a wider public of readers and practitioners. This was done through the so-called "public sphere" (Habermas 1962) which opened up new arenas of public debate (previously the exclusive domain of state and religious authorities) and encouraged critical argument based on reason and facts rather than subjective dogmas. The explosion of print culture at the time also made more information available to more people, meaning that participation in the public sphere was not only greater overall but also better informed (Headrick 2000).

In today's post-truth world, when some fear that Enlightenment values are coming under attack, it is possible to observe some interesting parallels. Once again, heightened scrutiny of expertise and new ways of interacting with information are coinciding with – and perhaps even catalysing – new approaches to public life. Experts are being encouraged to more visibly champion their contribution (and the contribution of evidence) to society, to be more transparent about what they do, and to more constructively recognise the limits of their knowledge. Cue evidence synthesis. Meanwhile, many are exploring new modes of engagement and ways of opening up elite, sometimes narrowly framed modes of enquiry. Cue public dialogue.

I have focussed on synthesis and dialogue as two important ways that science policy is already adapting, and can further adapt, to the post-truth challenge. But there are other opportunities being seized too.

In my own work I am witnessing an exciting burst of innovative methods to help more people to engage with evidence and complex ideas, and to engage in new ways. These include everything from novel uses of images, objects, and data-driven infographics to new approaches to modelling, gaming, and interdisciplinary practice, particularly between the arts and sciences. While it may no longer be productive to talk of CP Snow's (1959) two cultures of art and science, we might still consider the distinction between rationality and sentiment. Successful interactions between scientists and policymakers require a healthy mix of both, and these new modes of science policy have the potential to offer that mix.

Finally, the post-truth phenomenon is coinciding with new formulations of what it means to be a scientist or expert, with more inclusive language, campaigns, and other efforts to demonstrate the importance of science to everyone. New forms of activism are also taking hold. The April 2017 "March for Science" galvanised more than a million people in over 600 cities worldwide to stand up for science and evidence, to not be complacent in thinking decisions will be informed by facts, and to do so collectively and inclusively in the public sphere. The march might not have stopped Trump reneging on the Paris deal just a few months later, but it did raise awareness and send a strong message. It may even have contributed to there being fewer cuts in US public spending on scientific research than many feared and, in some cases, significant increases (Science 2018).

In these various ways, the post-truth phenomenon has arguably forced a healthy degree of introspection within science and policy communities. It has also put a premium on innovative methods – such as forms of synthesis and dialogue – that deliver inclusive, rigorous, transparent, accessible, and socially intelligent evidence for policy-making and public life. What a great time to be doing what I do.

References

Baker, T 2017, *Fake news: what is it, and how can we tackle it?* Nesta. Available from: www.nesta.org.uk/blog/fake-news-what-is-it-and-how-can-we-tackle-it/.

Chwalisz, C 2017, *The people's verdict: adding informed citizen voices to public decision-making*, Rowman & Littlefield International, London.

Donnelly CA, Boyd I, Campbell P, Craig C, Vallance P, Walport M, Whitty CJM, Woods E & Wormald C 2018, 'Four principles to make evidence synthesis more useful for policy', *Nature*, vol. 558, pp. 361–364.

Doubleday, R & Wilsdon, J (eds.) 2013, *Future directions for scientific advice in Whitehall*, Centre for Science and Policy, Cambridge.

Gibbons, M 1999, 'Science's new social contract with society', *Nature*, vol. 402, pp. C81–C84.

Habermas, J 1962, *The structural transformation of the public sphere*, Polity Press, Cambridge.

Headrick, DR 2000, *When information came of age*, Oxford University Press, New York.

Hopkins Van Mil 2018, *Potential uses for genetic technologies: dialogue and engagement research conducted for the Royal Society*, Hopkins Van Mil.

Jasanoff, S & Hurlbut, B 2018, 'A global observatory for gene editing', *Nature*, vol. 555, pp. 435–437.

Milman, O 2013, 'Top 20 things politicians need to know about science', *The Guardian*. Available from: www.theguardian.com/science/2013/nov/20/top-20-things-politicians-need-to-know-about-science.

Noveck, BS 2015, *Smart citizens, smarter state: the technologies of expertise and the future of governing*, Harvard University Press, Cambridge.

O'Neill, O 2013, *What we don't understand about trust*, TED.

Owens, S 2015, *Knowledge, policy and expertise*, Oxford University Press, Oxford.

Pagden, A 2013, *The Enlightenment and why it still matters*, Oxford University Press.

Peplow, M (ed.) 2014, *Innovation: managing risk, not avoiding it*, Government Office for Science, London.

Pidgeon, N & Henwood K 2014, 'Perceptions of risk', in *Innovation: managing risk, not avoiding it*, ed M Peplow, Government Office for Science, pp. 93–106.

Ramakrishnan, V 2017, *Potential and risks of recent developments in biotechnology*, The Royal Society.

Science 2018, 'Trump, Congress approve largest U.S. research spending increase in a decade'. *Science News*.

Scopus 2018, Content Coverage Guide. Elsevier. Available from: www.elsevier.com/__data/assets/pdf_file/0007/69451/0597-Scopus-Content-Coverage-Guide-US-LETTER-v4-HI-singles-no-ticks.pdf.

Snow, CP 1959, *The two cultures and the scientific revolution*, Cambridge University Press, Cambridge.

Stilgoe, J 2013, 'You can have too much precision', *The Guardian*. Available from: www.theguardian.com/science/political-science/2013/feb/12/too-much-precision.

Surowiecki, J 2005, *The wisdom of crowds: how the many are smarter than the few*, Abacus, London.

Sutherland, WJ & Burgman, M 2015, 'Policy advice: use experts wisely', *Nature*, vol. 526, pp. 317–318.

The Royal Society and the Academy of Medical Sciences 2018, *Evidence synthesis for policy*, The Royal Society.

The Royal Society 2017, *Machine learning: the power and promise of computers that learn by example*, The Royal Society.

Tesich, S 1992, 'A government of lies', *The Nation*. Available from: https://drive.google.com/file/d/0BynDrdYrCLNtdmt0SFZFeGMtZUFsT1NmTGVTQmcIdEpmUClz/view.

Tyler, C 2013, 'Top 20 things scientists need to know about policy-making', *The Guardian*.

van der Linden, S et al. 2017, 'Inoculating against misinformation', *Science*, vol. 358, no. 6367, pp. 1141–1142.

Whitty, CJM 2015, 'What makes an academic paper useful for health policy?', *BMC Medicine*, vol. 13, p. 301.

3 Trustworthiness, quality, and value

The regulation of official statistics in a post-truth age

Ed Humpherson

Introduction

The term 'post-truth' was awarded the prestigious accolade of the Oxford Dictionary's (2016) word of 2016. It defined post-truth as:

> Relating to or denoting circumstances in which objective facts are less influential in shaping public opinion than appeals to emotion or personal belief

The term spawned a mini-publication boom, with at least three books published in 2017 anatomising the phenomenon, by Matthew d'Ancona (*Post-truth: The New War on Truth and How to Fight Back*), Evan Davis (*Post Truth: Why we have reached peak bullshit and what we can do about it*), and James Ball (*Post-Truth: How Bullshit Conquered the World*).

The term came to be seen as embodying a threat to a range of established professions, including broadcast and print journalism, science, and my own profession of statistics. This chapter summarises how, as the standard-setter and regulator for UK official statistics, we have sought to respond to this range of threats. It will start by putting the term 'post-truth' in a broader context, and then outline two key institutional responses: creating a new regulatory body called the Office for Statistics Regulation and revising the Code of Practice for UK official statistics.

Post-truth and statistics

This is not the place to debate whether post-truth is merely an exaggeration of existing tendencies and trends in public discourse, or alternatively represents a new and worrying threat to the public realm.

Instead, this section will provide some broader context on the significance of post-truth for the world of statistics.

At one level, it does indeed appear to represent a profound threat. A growing debate about the reliability of 'facts' used in public debate could undermine confidence in the usefulness of statistics published by official bodies on a wide range of issues – health, crime, the economy, the environment, and so on. 'Post-truth' may reflect a depreciation of values like integrity in the use of evidence, recognition of the strengths and limitations of data, and the quality of data itself – in short, the values that underpin a system of official statistics.

But we see the debate on post-truth as a particular crystallisation, at a particular political moment, of a much broader range of trends that impact on the role of statistics and data in society. These include

- We are in a world that is increasingly rich in data. Data are abundantly available – easier to collect, easier to combine, easier to analyze, and easier to disseminate. In this data-rich world, the idea of official statistics as representing some unique standard may no longer be tenable. Lots of organisations can collect and publish statistics relatively easily. But a world of abundant data is also one where it is easier to select and highlight preferred data to suit a particular narrative, and one where a citizen can easily feel overwhelmed by the volume of competing assertions that are made using data.
- We are also in a world of increasing concern about the way in which personal data are processed and used, by both Government and private sector actors. This concern has been growing consistently for at least a decade and has been punctuated by key moments of convulsion: high profile data losses like care.data, Cambridge Analytica, and the robust regulatory response of Europe's General Data Protection Regulation.
- There is also a sense of expertise losing its cachet in society. It is difficult to discern whether this is a meaningfully distinct trend, or whether it is a continuation of a long-standing scepticism about and divide between experts of all kinds and the publics they seek to serve. What *is* clear is that people are concerned and talking about this as much as ever.

This chapter summarises changes in response to these factors to the governance of UK statistics. These changes involved the creation of a new Office for Statistics Regulation and the publication of a refreshed Code of Practice.

The UK's governance system

The UK has had a governance regime with independent scrutiny and assessment of statistics since 2007, under the Statistics and Registration Services Act (SRSA 2007). The Act gave the UK Statistics Authority the power to set a Code of Practice, assess compliance with the Code, award the designation of National Statistics, and monitor how far statistics are serving the public interest. In November 2016, the UK Statistics Authority relaunched the governance role through a new Office for Statistics Regulation.

The decision to create the Office for Statistics Regulation had as its immediate cause a major review of economic statistics conducted by Sir Charles Bean (HM Treasury 2016). The Bean Review of Economic Statistics considered the importance of improved statistics on the UK economy and among its recommendations was the proposal for a stronger, more separate identity for the Authority's regulatory function. But there were broader factors at play too in the decision to establish the Office. In major political debates in the period 2013 to 2016, statistics were playing an increasingly prominent role, including in understanding the UK's trading relationships and migration to the UK, the trajectory for living standards, and evidence on the efficiency of the housing market and the provision of health services. And the term 'post-truth' itself was a factor. We wanted to respond to the anxiety that, in a world of abundant data, appropriate use of and respect for statistics was under threat.

A new Office for Statistics Regulation

The Office for Statistics Regulation absorbed the regulatory functions of the Authority, which had previously been undertaken by a less visible team called Monitoring and Assessment. But there was no change in statutory function.

This begs a question: what was new? Was this simply a case of a cosmetic change in name? The answer is that, while the functions and powers are the same, there are significant changes in purpose and strategy. And these changes make all the difference.

The purpose of the Office for Statistics Regulation

Before launching the Office for Statistics Regulation, we spent a huge amount of time developing, refining, and agreeing an organisational purpose. We wanted to make sure the purpose was clear to staff, the

Board, the statistical community, and wider audiences like the media. Purpose was the crucial animating force that brought the whole process of creating the Office for Statistics Regulation together.

We recognised that the existing team – the Monitoring and Assessment team – lacked a clear statement of its role. Even the name 'Monitoring and Assessment' seemed to lack a focus, being both passive (to 'monitor' does not sound particularly dynamic) and vague (what is being monitoring and assessed?)

The purpose statement we agreed was:

> Statistics are an essential public asset. We enhance public confidence in the trustworthiness, quality and value of statistics produced by Government. We set the standards they must meet. We celebrate when the standards are met, and challenge publicly when they are not. We are champions of relevant statistics in a changing public world.
>
> (Office for Statistics Regulation 2018a)

Public, philosophy, and proportionality

Two main features of this purpose statement are:

- The emphasis on the public: the purpose is all about the public role of statistics. The phrase 'statistics are a public asset' represents a core belief of the office – that statistics are not produced for elites (experts, policymakers) but for citizens. The word 'public' appears four times in the purpose.
- The balance of celebrating and challenging: it was important to communicate that we are not simply here to criticise poor production and use of statistics – though we are not shy of doing so where necessary. We also celebrate statistics when they do a great job of serving the public – through the National Statistics designation and by highlighting great work when we see it.

Value: from a mechanical to a social view of statistics

The purpose statement gives equal weight to the *value* of statistics as to the process of production (trustworthiness) and to quality – which had been the focus of assessment of statistics before the creation of the Office. This emphasis on value sends a very important signal: it is not enough to produce high-quality statistics in a well-managed way. Statistics must also be useful to users. They must be accessible, meet user needs, provide insight, and answer user questions. This raises the stakes for Government statisticians – they cannot simply publish a set of numbers and think their job is done. They must also provide insight, by connecting to the questions and interests of their audiences. The focus on value de-emphasises the mechanical and priorities the social communication aspects of statistics – a profound change in perspective.

Happy families

From this focus on value flows another consequence. The preceding Monitoring and Assessment team tended to focus on individual statistics, by reviewing whether they complied with the Code of Practice. This remains a central role of the new Office. The focus on value requires us to widen our focus to consider families or systems of statistics. The focus on groups of statistics shed light on broader questions about society: how well are people treated by the health service? What is happening to jobs and wages? And societal questions like this cannot be answered by just one set of statistics. Instead one needs to consider 'families' of statistics, in which each 'member' captures different aspects of a question. So the Office for Statistics Regulation now focusses on reviews of the value of groups or families of statistics.

But the main product of this new Office has been a refreshed Code of Practice focussed on supporting public confidence in statistics, to which this chapter now turns.

A new Code of Practice

In the UK, the *Code of Practice for Official Statistics* has been at the heart of setting high standards for official statistics. The first edition of the Code was published by the UK Statistics Authority in January 2009 as one of the Statistics Authority's statutory responsibilities under the UK's Statistics and Registration Service Act[1].

Since then, the UK's Code has established itself as the heart of the UK's system of official statistics. It has been adopted widely across the UK public sector, within over 150 bodies who publish official statistics. It forms the basis of the assessment of statistics by the Office for Statistics Regulation and leads to the award of the National Statistics designation.

In 2015, we launched a stocktake. This stocktake reviewed how the Code was working in practice. The stocktake concluded that we should consult on a revised version of the Code.

The code and post-truth

The features of the post-truth world noted above came together to create the case for change. We became concerned that widespread debate about the reliability of political statements might infect public confidence in official statistics. We wanted to issue a strong response that defended the value of official statistics.

We also needed to recognise the impact of data abundance and to reflect much greater concern about the trustworthiness of organisations who hold private information on individuals.

And we recognised a gradual shift from concerns about organisational process to concerns about statistical quality. In 2008, when the original Code was developed, concerns surrounded the processes of production – so things like pre-release access, organisational governance, and publication policies were at the core of the 2008 Code. By 2015 and 2016, the focus of concern was shifting away from these basics of production and towards quality. Concerns emerged at roughly the same time in different sectors, including crime statistics (with criticism of the reliability of recording of crimes by the police, which undermined confidence in aggregate statistics on crime); migration statistics (with growing Parliamentary criticism of the survey-based approach to measuring net migration to the UK); and most prominently, the Bean review of economic statistics, which highlighted issues with the quality of economic statistics.

The walled garden

The final factor was more endogenous: the culture created by the first version of the Code itself. While this Code had been very successful in setting standards across the UK public sector and in providing the basis to protect statistics from political interference, in some ways it may have done its job too well. The first version of the Code came to be seen as a barrier to innovation in some Government Departments, and this, in turn, could damage public confidence. It led us to lament that official statistics were starting to resemble a 'walled garden' – beautiful, well looked after, but elitist and cut off from the world outside, and not consistent with public confidence.

Our approach: focus on public confidence

We recognised a key distinction between the Code's users and its beneficiaries. The **users** of the Code are those people who draw on the Code on a regular basis to guide decisions about the production of official statistics – people who work in organisations that produce official statistics, including statisticians, policymakers, and communications professionals. The Code's **beneficiaries** are a much wider group of people who benefit from statistics. These beneficiaries include people with a role in public policy; expert users who undertake research, business, and community groups who draw on statistics to make decisions; and – perhaps most importantly – the broader public who want to be reassured about the reliability of the statistics on which public decisions and discourse are based.

The human factor

We wanted to put public confidence at the heart of the new Code. But what does this mean in practice? We started to identify the general factors that underpinned confidence in any exchange of information, and it gradually become clearer that in an exchange of information between human beings, the quality of the information itself is only one of the things that supports confidence. The identity and reliability of the provider of the information is equally important and, in many situations, precedes any focus on the information's quality: a person is hardly likely to inspect in detail the quality of a statement made by someone who is known to be a liar.

This analysis led us, in turn, to identify three attributes of data and statistics that are necessary to achieve public confidence:

- The trustworthiness of the provider of the information.
- The quality of the information.
- The value of the information to the user.

The three pillars

Through an iterative process of consultation, we developed these ideas into three pillars which form the basis of the new Code:

- **Trustworthiness:** Trustworthiness is about the processes, people, and systems of organisations. It is based on the ideas of Baroness Onora O'Neill around trust and trustworthiness (O'Neill 2002). As Sir David Spiegelhalter said in his President's Address to the Royal Statistical Society in July 2017, 'no-one can just expect to be trusted' (Spiegelhalter 2017). An organisation must provide testable evidence to demonstrate that they have the interests of the public at heart, by demonstrating competence, honesty, and openness. The practices under the Trustworthiness pillar set out the key commitments that must be made to support independent statistics production.

- **Quality** is about the data and how they are processed into statistics. Following the Bean Review of Economic Statistics, the Code recognises that the independence of production is not, on its own, enough to guarantee worthwhile statistics. The statistics must be the best available estimate of what they aim to measure, and should not mislead. To achieve this the data must be relevant, the methods must be sound, and the assurance around the outputs must be clear. These aspects of statistical production are at the heart of the practices in the Quality pillar.

- **Value** follows the emphasis in the UN Fundamental Principles of Official Statistics on statistics that 'meet the test of practical utility' (United Nations 2013). It defines what statistics must provide for the public. This includes a coherent picture, a focus on users, an emphasis on what questions the statistics answer, and a focus on innovation as the world changes. Trustworthy processes to create high-quality data may not be useful to the public if the statistics are not accessible, do not address key questions, are inefficiently produced, and do not add value or provide insight.

These pillars are conceptually distinct. But they support each other. A producer of official statistics is more likely to be perceived as trustworthy where the data they provide are clearly of high quality. High-quality statistics are much more likely to provide useful answers to key questions than lower-quality statistics.

We published the new Code on February 22, 2018 (UK Statistics Authority 2018). It was built around the three pillars, supported by 14 principles (each supported by detailed practices), as shown in Figure 3.1.

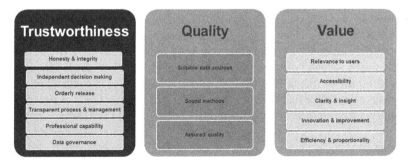

Figure 3.1 The three pillars and 14 principles of the UK's new Code of Practice.

Voluntary adoption

We also wanted to expand the Code's reach. In a world of abundant data and multiple data sources, the pillars of trustworthiness, quality, and value have broader application. They can support public confidence in a much wider range of data outputs than just official statistics, and from a wider range of producers – not all of them in Government.

From this insight, we have developed the concept of voluntary adoption of the Code. We encourage organisations that publish research and analysis, both inside and outside Government, to adopt a 'review and publish' approach. They should review their practices against the Code – how do they assure themselves of the quality of their data; what is the value of what they produce; and how do they demonstrate a trustworthy process – and they can then publish short statements alongside their data or research explaining how they line up to the three pillars. Several organisations have already adopted the Code voluntarily, including:

- The Race Disparity Unit (RDU 2018), which publishes data on a website highlighting different outcomes from public services for different ethnicities.
- The Scottish Fiscal Commission (2018), which forecasts Scottish Gross Domestic Product (GDP) and tax revenues.
- The Department for Work and Pensions (2018), which adopted the Code on a voluntary basis for a range of publications.
- The Greater London Assembly (2018), which adopted the Code in July 2018.
- To support voluntary adoption of the Code, we have published a guide to voluntary adoption of the Code (Office for Statistics Regulation 2018b).

Conclusion

In a data-rich world, public confidence in data and analysis – in trustworthiness, quality, and value – is too important to be abandoned. A new body with a clear purpose, and a clear philosophy based on trustworthiness, quality, and value, has been an essential part of the response to a cluster of fears triggered by data abundance – fears which go beyond the simple neologism of post-truth. In the face of these fears, we believe the Office for Statistics Regulation and the new Code of Practice mark a step change in the governance of statistics in the UK.

Note

1 Section 10 of the Statistics and Registration Services Act 2007.

References

Department of Work and Pensions 2018, *Guidance: benefit expenditure and caseload tables*. Available from: www.gov.uk/government/publications/benefit-expenditure-and-caseload-tables-information-and-guidance/benefit-expenditure-and-caseload-tables-information-and-guidance.

Greater London Assembly 2018, *Code of practice for statistics*. Available from: www.london.gov.uk/about-us/governance-and-spending/code-practice-statistics-voluntary-application.

HM Treasury 2016, *Independent review of UK economic statistics*. Available from: https://assets.publishing.service.gov.uk/government/uploads/system/uploads/attachment_data/file/507081/2904936_Bean_Review_Web_Accessible.pdf.

Office for Statistics Regulation 2018a, *Business plan 2018/2019*. Available from: www.statisticsauthority.gov.uk/wp-content/uploads/2018/04/Business_Plan_201819.pdf.

Office for Statistics Regulation 2018b, *Building confidence in statistics*. Available from: www.statisticsauthority.gov.uk/code-of-practice/.

O'Neill, O 2002, Reith lectures 2002: a question of trust, lecture 4: trust & transparency. *BBC Reith Lectures*. Available from: www.bbc.co.uk/radio4/reith2002.

Oxford Dictionaries 2016, *Word of the year*. Available from: https://en.oxforddictionaries.com/word-of-the-year/word-of-the-year-2016.

Racial Disparity Unit 2018, *Statement of compliance with the code for practice for statistics*. Available from: www.ethnicity-facts-figures.service.gov.uk/static/statement-of-compliance.pdf.

Scottish Fiscal Commission 2018, *Compliance with the code for practice for official statistics*. Available from: www.fiscalcommission.scot/media/1229/scottish-fiscal-commission-voluntary-compliance-with-statistics-code-of-practice.pdf.

Spiegelhalter, D 2017, 'Trust in numbers', *Journal of the Royal Statistical Society: Series A (Statistics in Society)*, vol. 180, no. 4, pp. 948–965.

Statistics and Registration Services Act SRSA, 2007, *UK Statistics Authority*, London, UK. Available from: www.statisticsauthority.gov.uk/wp-content/uploads/2015/12/images-statisticsandregistrationserviceact2007_tcm97-18260.pdf.

UK Statistics Authority 2018, *Code of practice*. Available from: www.statisticsauthority.gov.uk/code-of-practice/.

United Nations 2013, *Fundamental principles of official statistics*. Economic and Social Council. United Nations. Available from: https://unstats.un.org/unsd/dnss/gp/FP-Rev2013-E.pdf.

4 Risk and uncertainty in the context of government decision-making

Ian L. Boyd

Introduction

In this chapter, I will present a view of how risk manifests in government and how it is managed. This view has been based on experience as a Senior Civil Servant in the UK Government and Chief Scientific Adviser to the UK Government on food and environment. In that context, for several years, I had responsibility for oversight of risk management in the UK Department for Environment, Food and Rural Affairs. This emerged because the department happened to be presented with a number of unprecedented events which it struggled to manage effectively and there was a perception that it had to improve its capacity to manage its risks.

A significant lesson from this experience is that risk, at least in the context of government, is mostly a social construct (Sitkin & Pablo 1992). Risk is as much a matter of perception as it is of problems set within physical reality (sometimes referred to as 'real' as opposed to 'perceived' risk, see Sitkin & Pablo 1992). The timing and circumstances of an event can be more important in the evolution of risk than the actual physical manifestation of that risk. The best evidence to support this conclusion was that few of the risks I identified were ever successfully managed out of existence; all that happened was that extant risks were either sequentially down-graded when they were replaced with even bigger and more dangerous risks or balanced off by new opportunities which arose by chance rather than by design as part of a risk management process. When ash disease invaded the UK in 2012, this set off a significant public reaction (Urquhart et al. 2017), but six years later, the real risk from this disease had not abated. It appeared as just one of many hundreds of equivalent risks on the UK risk register of invasive plant pathogens. The perception of the risk had changed in the intervening time rather than the risk itself.

It is therefore important to understand that risk, at least within government, has strong cognitive elements. If managers in government have skill and confidence in sufficient measure then risk is greatly diminished. This is not just because risk is so often about perception but also because the management of risk is a dynamic, embedded process which calls on the collective intuition of the executive to manage effectively. In other words, good managers will probably also be good risk managers even without the help of formalised risk management processes.

Of course, no amount of bravado or innate skill compensates for governments not having a strong risk management framework. In 2017, the UK government published its framework (Cabinet Office 2017) – surprisingly the first one for such a mature government system – and this is accompanied by a detailed description of how an advanced government considers risk and uncertainty should be factored into decision-making (HM Treasury 2013). It is not my aim to summarise or recapitulate this because, overall, it follows the standard architecture of most large corporate risk management systems.

Instead I will attempt to provide a framework for thinking about risk in government from a systems perspective and then focus on environmental risk and its importance, because that is my interest. I will then consider how people in government perceive risk and how they then structure their risk portfolios and, in effect, share risk between themselves and the civil societies they help to manage and represent. I will then suggest what I believe is the only viable framework for decision-making when there is high risk and uncertainty. This leads to an analysis of why I think the Precautionary Principle, which is one approach to risk management, is subservient to the principle of proportionality because the former is only a special case of the latter. Proportionality has much more practical application to risk-based decision-making in government. Finally, I will consider disaster risk management which is right at the sharp end of what governments are expected to do on behalf of citizens.

A systems perspective on risk in governments

Risk is usually described as the product of the severity of a hazard and its likelihood of occurrence. Extreme hazards are often low risk because we have effective ways of controlling them, but some low hazards can be high risk because they are uncontrolled. Examples of these extremes for governments might be the effects of severe storms and the effects of air pollution, respectively. However, risk mainly arises because of our uncertainties about the world around us. If we lived in a deterministic world, where uncertainty is eliminated, then we could learn to control all our risks. Unfortunately the world is not like this, and much of the effort of natural and social science is focussed on reducing the uncertainties about the world and, as a result, enabling us to control risk.

These investigative efforts recognise that, in practice, the job of government is often defined as the management of systems (Boyd 2016), such as the economy, food production or distribution, or waste. All these kinds of systems can have low predictability about how they will change or evolve in future, so the job of government becomes systems management under conditions of high uncertainty. Much of the risk experienced by government is because of system uncertainty, and narrowing this uncertainty requires these managed systems to be understood in greater detail based on both natural science and social science. Sometimes, however, systems managed by government are more or less chaotic, meaning that the system dynamics are inherently unpredictable, so additional scientific knowledge cannot help to constrain the risk management problem.

Attractors, state-shifts, and tipping points

Typically, the systems managed by government tend to have non-linear dynamics because the processes which result in system operation do not have simple cause-effect relationships. This means it is insufficient to know the inputs to the system in order to predict the behaviour of the system measured in terms of its outputs. Multiple causation is normal, and the relationships between components of a governed system are usually both non-linear and statistically non-stationary. However, most systems have some level of in-built stability in that they oscillate around a central point (it's 'attractor'), so they will usually tend to produce outputs which have some level of broad predictability. For example, food commodity prices, though volatile, tend to oscillate around a mean, largely because of the stabilising mechanisms, or feedbacks, which regulate supply and demand. If the world was not built in this way, then life as we know it would not be possible. It is this process which give us governments themselves because the social system from which we derive statehood results in semi-stable entities like national governments with their fractal substructures and subsystems.

Governments rely on this stabilising property of systems to allow them to apparently manage the systems for which they have responsibility with a degree of perceived control. Arguably, it is the job of

· governments to attempt to sustain the systems they manage around a single attractor or, if not, to shift the system to oscillate around another attractor using directed policy interventions.

The overall risk carried by governments, therefore, is a property of the system structure. Mathematical representations of highly networked systems show that system complexity sometimes, although not always, begets greater stability because there are more feedbacks creating checks and balances, thus preventing system collapse. This process builds in self-regulation or a tendency towards homeostasis.

A question still to be answered is whether evolved systems have greater stability and resilience, and therefore lower levels of inherent risk, than bespoke engineered systems. Like organisms, which are evolved systems, the answer to this is probably that governments do carry less risk if they have been allowed to evolve their governance machinery (people, statute, institutions, relationships) over long periods of time.

Without structural systemic stability, the aggregate risk carried by governments could change quickly when faced with a novel set of challenges. This would be equivalent to an organism experiencing environmental conditions beyond its physiological tolerance leading to distress. For example, the risks carried by the UK government in relation to Brexit might fall into this class of rapid and novel change which is shifting the systems managed. In this case, a mature government might be able to weather the aggregate risk in a way that would be a considerable challenge to a less mature, or less evolved, government.

If governed systems are stressed this may result in the exceedance of thresholds of behaviour and switches of system state (tipping points). At small scales, these kinds of behaviours carry epithets such as 'the law of unintended consequences' or 'perverse outcomes'. The elasticity of the system will determine how quickly a stressed system returns to oscillate around its original state, or attractor, but there is a risk that a system may switch to oscillating around a different point of attraction, sometimes known as a *state shift*. I think this is what we are seeing in relation to Brexit in the UK. Elections can also bring different governments to power which have radically different ideas about how to manage an economy or how civil society should be structured and this kind of shift could result in a state shift in the economy or social system of a country. There are also other kinds of shifts in system state often imposed by natural processes (e.g., volcanic activity, earthquakes, sea level rise, disease epidemics, and extreme climate) or even by the internal dynamics of the system, sometimes fuelled by stochastic political processes. Risk arises when these internal dynamics potentially affect a particular course of action or preferred system state.

Aleatory and epistemic risk

These risks can either be reduced by increasing knowledge – known as epistemic risk – or they are part of the noise which exists within the dynamics of the systems being managed by government – known as aleatory risk. In reality governments deal with both types of risks but often do not distinguish clearly between them. Governments can systematically reduce the epistemic component of risk by filling gaps in knowledge through research or by changing the machinery of government, or improving the skills of those involved in government, to make government more efficient in the face of risks. However, often the high costs of filling knowledge gaps and improving efficiency means that a lot of epistemic risk is not managed out of the system. There is also nothing governments can do about the aleatory component of risk; it is the irreducible noise within the semi-chaotic systems they manage. As a result, the administrative systems within government are usually constructed to cope with chronic levels of moderate and high epistemic risk.

In my experience, government managers often try to manage irreducible aleatory risk as if it is reducible epistemic risk. For example, it is well known that government business cases contain high levels of optimism bias (Weinstein & Klein 1996). This happens because civil servants are incentivised to present business cases which work and not spend a lot of time on business cases that do not work. Risks emerge from this optimism bias because initiatives will often not deliver the benefits envisaged. Treating this as epistemic risk – 'we just need better business cases' – misses the point. If the behaviours involved in producing business cases, which are biased about the benefits, are deeply embedded in the psyche of the civil servants, or the civil service itself, then it is irreducible aleatory risk. Better training and improved guidance and oversight might eventually reduce this kind of risk, but it is likely to emerge from basic and irreducible human frailty. Understanding this will inform different kinds of solutions.

Foundational risks and the environment

Foundational risk is defined here as risk which happens because of potential failure in an early part of the chain of causation. It follows that recognising and managing risks which occur early in this chain can have widespread benefits.

Risk, as it relates to government, can be broadly categorised into cognitive types, such as economic, financial, political, social, safety and security, and environmental. There is a strong case for placing environmental risks as a common foundational component of this risk architecture. This is because the environment is the most ubiquitous and least controlled of the inputs to the systems managed by governments. It is also an emerging driver of inequality (Brulle & Pellow 2006) and safety and security risks (Burke et al. 2009).

The environment supplies the basics of life – clean water and air, and nutritious food – as well as many other secondary components including security from disease and extreme weather and geological events. For governments this translates into a plethora of management tasks all of which have high levels of uncertainty. Directed investments in infrastructure and people, mostly over many decades or even centuries, have helped to reduce the risks associated with these uncertainties. For example, most of the rivers flowing through major cities in the developed world have been the subject of continuous investments to control flood risk.

However, new risks are emerging all the time. Anti-microbial resistance (World Health Organization 2015) is one such risk which has risen up government agendas in the past decade, but there are many others concerning security which are highly dynamic and which require agility of response delivered by specialised parts of government.

A rising environmental risk comes from waste and pollution. This has been recognised as an existential risk for many centuries, but the acceleration of resource consumption married with the invention of new materials has outgrown the planetary capacity to absorb and process many waste outputs. This is creating a risk to the availability of clean air and water, and nutritious food. These feedbacks from the process of human consumption have considerable implications for human health and equality with consequences for political stability and international security. Environmental productivity, in terms of both how much energy can be produced in raw form or as food and the capacity of the environment to absorb the outputs from consumption without poisoning the energy generation process, are the foundational risks faced by people and the planet. Consequently, they are foundational risks for national governments, even if they are not always explicitly acknowledged. Environmental risks can propagate down the chain of causation as other forms of risk especially those concerning security (Burke et al. 2009; Maystadt, Tan & Breisinger 2014). Despite this governments tend to spend most of their time and resources managing risks which are distal to this and other similar foundations.

The process of risk management in government

It is often difficult to get those who work within government to take the concept of risk seriously and especially to recognise a risk hierarchy – i.e., some risks are foundational, while other risks are consequential – in spite of such hierarchies being deeply embedded in risk management procedures (CDC 2017). For example, defence spending is usually prioritised relative to spending to mitigate environmental and other risks which are the sources of security problems.

Risk indifference in government

This happens for three main reasons. The first is that those who run government – civil servants – when challenged to adopt more explicit risk management will often explain their jobs are primarily concerned with managing risks so the development of a risk-based architecture is seen as an unnecessary feature of government because they see risk management as completely integral to what governments do. The problem with this is that they often do not see beyond the narrow operational risks owned by them.

The second reason is that the very processes of making risk explicit in government can increase the likelihood and severity of some risks. At its simplest, sections of the public might be alarmed if it was to see the risk assessments associated with some parts of the systems managed by government on its behalf. In this circumstance, why would one create a new risk by talking explicitly about risks? This is a Catch 22. We are very conscious about how financial markets respond to the slightest hint of changing risk from the financial managers within governments. I have referred above to these non-linearities in system response. In some cases, controlling these non-linearities may involve not being explicit about risk.

The third reason is that the political component of government often sees risk differently from the business managers within government. Managing political risk can require quite different solutions from transactional or naturally occurring risks. Politicians are often attempting to call out risk or can be actively magnifying risk to gain advantage.

An apparent indifference to risk, or perhaps a paralysis about knowing how to manage risk which is manifest as indifference, is common in government.

Strategic and operational risk

Risk can be subdivided into operational, or transactional, risk or strategic risk involving broad and long-term risks.

Operational risks include legal, delivery, reputational, financial, and natural risks. Most of the risks carried by governments fall within one or more of these categories. Natural risk, such as the risk of food contamination, is what most people would normally expect to see being managed by governments. But governments are also continually having to contend with legal challenges to their decisions and their operational management, and there are risks that they could be found to operating outside the law. The activities carried out by government may fail, or there can be failure in financial management. However, perhaps more than anything governments need to manage reputational risk (Larkin 2003). This is the risk associated with not being seen to do a good job of managing other risks, and politics, together with communications, can play a significant part in how risk is either dampened down or amplified.

But if governments fail to recognise and manage their strategic risks, then they will be ill-prepared and will often fail to make the major, long-term investments in infrastructure like hospitals, power generation, schools, forests, carbon sequestration, and transport to respond to slow-moving risks, such as changing climate, demographic trends, and patterns of work.

One of the most important reasons for government maintaining risk registers is to properly document strategic risks. These often run counter to the ways in which the public prioritises risk (Weber 2006), and unless strategic risks are defined explicitly they are easily bypassed because it is often politically more important to manage operational risk. Failure to understand and manage strategic risk tends to magnify or create operational risks in the first place. Mature and confident government will spend a greater proportion of its time managing strategic risk because this is the way that governments get themselves ahead of problems and invest in the future in order to reduce future risk and cost. Effective foresight and horizon scanning analysis is a central feature of strategic risk planning. While the UK government does some of this (e.g., Government Office for Science 2018), the effectiveness of this kind of risk and opportunity analysis depends on how it then informs strategy. The strength of this link from foresight analysis to strategy, and then to effective implementation, varies greatly across government and also through time depending on the quality of the political leadership.

Strategic risks have a lot in common with foundational risks mentioned previously. For example, in Britain the management of the operational risk associated with the National Health Service will be improved if there is a greater emphasis on managing the sources of illness. The latter would require a very different long-term focus on issues like environmental quality, diet, and lifestyle, but very few governments in Britain have ever managed to dig themselves out of the hole associated with just pouring increasing amounts of resource into healthcare provision to mitigate proximate health risks rather than switching to reducing the sources of illness by dealing with ultimate causes.

This problem arises from the attitudes and skills of those within government, referred at the beginning of this section. Government managers often lose sight of strategic risks because of their focus on proximate rather than ultimate causation.

A further mistake often made in some parts of government is to assume that strategic risks emerge from the aggregation of many operational risks. This usually emerges from the implementation of systems of risk management which are vertically integrated through the corporate management structure like government departments. Simply taking operational risks and aggregating them at each level in the organisation rarely says much about strategic risk and almost always reflects current and past rather than future risk. Good strategic risk identification emerges from horizon scanning or foresight analyses. Governments probably underinvest chronically in the strategic story telling which can better prepare them for future challenges.

Risk management in practice – risk sharing

There is evidence that governments spend money to reduce their risks (Rodrik 1998), but governments would be hamstrung if they were perpetually the insurer of first resort, so sharing risk with others and, therefore, sharing the costs of risk management is a significant part of good governance. Mature government will have developed sophisticated methods of risk sharing. Significant parts of the functions of government are designed to adjust the balance of liabilities accruing to the state (public liabilities) as opposed to individuals, companies, and institutions (private liabilities). The public liabilities are indemnified through general taxation, while the private liabilities are indemnified either through privately held risk or they are shared through the purchase of insurance.

Government often uses regulation to adjust where the burden of risk lies, but regulation itself is often a blunter and less effective instrument for achieving risk sharing than voluntary and non-statutory methods (Barth, Caprio & Levine 2002). Sharing risks with those who are most closely associated with generating the risks also has the benefit of mitigating risks by holding to account those responsible for generating the risks in the first place, and this can be a way of changing behaviours to better manage, or even eliminate, the risks. This is often done by means of economic and social coercion rather than direct penalties. For example, the reputational impacts of risks to human health from food are sufficient to ensure that major retailers, rather than government, invest in food quality assurance.

The extent to which governments can manage their own risks by shifting responsibility depends on circumstances. When those who are largely responsible for generating the risks are individual citizens (voters) risk sharing becomes more challenging than when regulated businesses are involved. For example, governments find it difficult to charge citizens for the weight of waste they generate but have much less difficulty doing this for businesses. In some areas, such as waste management, there tends to be less enthusiasm within individual citizens for shouldering their own burden of risk because the state has taken this burden from them and they are reluctant to take on more risk. Conversely, the state does not carry the burden of risk of road accidents and requires drivers to carry that burden themselves. Arguably, in situations where the state takes on the burden this reduces options to incentivise changes in behaviours which might reduce or eliminate risk, suggesting that there are advantages to civil society from government not owning many risks.

The case of domestic waste management also illustrates that the charges placed on citizens by the state, levied through taxation, are rarely sufficient to properly insure for the risks underlying the promises made by politicians to win votes. This is a problem also illustrated by the risk from air pollution. Most (although not all) industrial sources of air pollution are well controlled by regulation, but governments are reluctant to shift responsibility for the risks caused by air pollution coming from vehicle emissions to individual vehicle drivers and to hold them to account for their portion of the aggregate risk to human health from their own activities. The result is that there is a very large cost to pay for the human health burden of air pollution, largely sitting within the budget of the National Health Service, which is not shared evenly across the population.

Sharing risk through markets

However, there are certain risks which only government can manage. Both local and central governments often manage the kinds of risk which most other organisations would reject on the basis of their magnitude. This is a form of market failure, and much of the process of government can be focussed on attempting to address this kind of market failure in risk sharing. Governments will attempt to reduce its liabilities by encouraging the development of insurance markets, such as the reinsurance options for home insurance against flooding in the UK (known as 'Flood Re'), which required legislation to create the right circumstances for the market to work. Without this, government would be left holding the risk as the UK government found to its cost during the banking crisis of 2008.

Another example of risk reduction by governments through sharing within markets comes from the way in which governments insure themselves against food security risks by investing in building effective global food markets. This relies on the diversity of supply, in terms of both sources and supply chains, to buffer against shortages or supply chain disruption rather than the storage of food close to the point of consumption. This requires considerable faith in market mechanisms to mitigate the risks, but not all governments have this faith, and some, such as China and Germany, maintain stores of some basic commodities as insurance against food security risks (however, it turns out that this behaviour creates a set of new risks, so it is not necessarily a response which indemnifies the government involved).

The risk of unshared risk

The extent to which risk sharing happens depends on the specific sectors of government business. There are clearly issues, such as managing the risk to national security, which are better to organise and fund within government. This is an example of the 'command and control' approach by governments to risk management. The market approach is at the opposite end of a spectrum of the scale of government intervention and covers most aspects of economic activity. Where the risks are large, governments can struggle to find the right balance between these opposites. Food production in Europe was designed after Second World War (WWII) to sustain food supplies. The security of supply was, and remains, a part of the rationale for the Common Agricultural Policy although this doctrine is now being challenged (Galtier 2013). Rather than letting the farming industry develop under normal business and market rules, complex mechanisms have been developed to subsidise the existence of farming in some places even though it is highly inefficient.

The cultures of dependency engendered in farmers supported by state-based subsidies have been embedded structurally in some parts of the European farming system. Therefore, the resolution of one risk through government intervention involving food security has ultimately lead to increased rather than reduced risk of food insecurity. Arguably this has been the major ultimate cause of Britain having the greatest epidemic of bovine tuberculosis (TB) of any developed country. By not sharing risk, government has brought upon itself an unmanageable burden. Many of the problems of low farm productivity in Britain can probably be tracked back to the same ultimate cause involving low levels of risk sharing by government.

The management of risk in this context intersects with political philosophy and the role of the state. Nationalised infrastructure and services are all very well, but this leads to shifting the burden of risk on to government and reduces the effectiveness of market mechanisms for risk sharing.

Risk accounting

Risk management across government would be enhanced greatly by better risk accounting. Risk accounting is a term applied mainly in financial management rather than across all of government. The insurance industry provides some market-based information concerned with risk accountancy, but this normally only deals with market-based risks and generally excludes government risk. The overall risk carried by governments is also probably reflected in the yield on government bonds (Diebold 2006), but there could be much debate about how well this prices risk or how useful this information is to those who actually manage risk in government.

Economic analysis involving quantification of costs and benefits of different decisions often verges on risk accounting at the level of transactional business decisions, but risk accounting is insufficiently mature to be able effectively to measure the balance of aggregated risk held by government as opposed to that held privately by non-government individuals and organisations. For example, there is no overall picture of how risk is distributed across national economies.

Risk accountancy could provide a better general appreciation of the level of liability held by society in general and the proportion of this which is accountable to government. This could provide a better measure than is currently available to justify the burden of taxation at local and national levels. It would also allow national governments to set strategic objectives about their preferred balance of risk liability.

Decision-making under uncertainty

At an operational level, government is always having to make decisions against a background of uncertainty. When the British government decided to cull badgers as a way of controlling bovine TB in the countryside it had no certainty that the intervention would work. What is the rational construct within which such risky decisions are made?

The epidemiology of TB in cattle, badgers, and the wider countryside is highly uncertain (Godfray et al. 2013). This means it is impossible to know in advance precisely how to control the spread of TB. To minimise the risk of the disease spreading, it is necessary to design an operational method for disease control which is built upon the most up-to-date information but to always expect that this will often not work as predicted. Decisions about how to proceed emerge from a process which synthesises across recent experiences (sometimes codified as information in publications or data), the corporate knowledge of those who carry out, manage, and supervise culling, and historical knowledge mostly from the published and peer-reviewed scientific literature and open-access Government reports. This results in a projection of what the consequences of any particular set of policy interventions might look like. The only way to find out whether this projection is correct is by testing it in an operational setting, assessing the outcome against the projected expectation and then learning from this experience.

This is not very different from the scientific process which involves developing a prior belief, or expectation or hypothesis, of what some aspect of the world will be like in future based upon current knowledge; this prior expectation is then confronted by the true future state once that emerges, and based on this new information it is then possible to further update our expectation of what the future will be like. This is also known as learning by experience or, in the context of a policy, 'adaptive management'. It is in my opinion the only effective method of managing complex processes under high risk and uncertainty, and it is normally how policy is implemented, even if this often happens without the explicit intent of those involved.

Adaptive management

Adaptive management is at the heart of risk management where there is high uncertainty. It is the intuitive way in which individuals and institutions operate to find out what works, and it has the advantage that it tracks the shifting variables in a complex and, perhaps, wicked problem. Wicked problems are ubiquitous risks in government, and they occur in circumstances where the very fact that a risk is being controlled can result in the nature of the risk itself changing. They are most common where there are strong social components at play and they generally occur because there is no consensus about why the problem in question should be tamed. This is in the nature of many disputes involving two or more parties with mutually incompatible objectives and no latitude to compromise.

There are two significant problems with the implementation of the adaptive management of risk. First, while those involved in making government decisions are often partial to being guided by such a framework, many are not so inclined which means that there can be patchy implementation. In most policy areas, adaptive management is a long-term approach which has to be carried through by different individuals. Unless the method of adaptive management is deeply embedded in the policy process, and the skills of civil servants, it can get lost at some point along the trajectory towards delivery.

Second, where political capital has been invested in a particular outcome, it is often difficult to explain that the outcome is uncertain, especially to those who may have to pay a cost because of the policy. This was the case with badger culling to control TB where there was considerable controversy and many stakeholders demanded certainty of the outcome before it got their support. This pushed politicians to start making promises which they might not keep because of the uncertainties inherent in the process they were managing. Consequently, in these cases adaptive management can amplify political risk and is often not popular with politicians.

Nevertheless, adaptive management introduces elements of the scientific process into decision-making and operational delivery within government. It emulates Bayesian updating so has its roots in statistical theory.

Precaution versus proportionality

A popular strategic approach to risk reduction in government is to invest in scientific research and innovation. However, in his report on innovation and risk (Government Office for Science 2014), Mark

Walport pointed out that innovation and risk were positively correlated. Progress driven through innovation, therefore, may solve problems and reduce risk, but it also carries the risk of generating new risks, and this is an inherent part of progress. In contrast, in the publication on '*late lessons from early warnings*' (European Environment Agency 2001), the European Environment Agency suggested that innovation itself should be avoided in order to reduce risk. Although the two publications agreed about the fundamental relationship between risk and innovation, they took opposite views about how to manage the relationship.

This contrast defines the difference between risk-based decision-making (Walport) and hazard-based decision-making (European Environment Agency) (Lofstedt 2011). Risk-based decision-making is an application of a *proportionality principle,* whereas in hazard-based decision-making, there is an application of a *Precautionary Principle.* The proportionality principle is defined by decisions based upon assessments of cost and benefit. When the costs are considered to be greater than the benefits, a particular innovation is probably not worth pursuing. The Precautionary Principle is actually just a special case of the proportionality principle which applies when there is insufficient information to carry out a rational cost-benefit analysis.

Lack of clarity in these definitions, or how they have been applied, has been at the centre of a lot of very poor decision-making by governments. In 2000, the European Commission tried to tie down the definition of the Precautionary Principle, which is embedded in European Law (European Commission 2000), but successive judgements by the European Court of Justice (ECJ) have, in effect, undermined the initial definition by countermanding the role of proportionality and establishing it as a hazard- rather than risk-based principle (Lofstedt 2014). Resorting to precaution – essentially a risk-free, hazard-based process for decision-making as redefined by the ECJ – means that it becomes very difficult for innovation to thrive. This stifles progress in ways that would be less likely under a principle of proportionality where risk is a more important part of decision-making. Ironically, application of the Precautionary Principle, which is just another form of designed risk avoidance, is likely only to shift risk elsewhere and perhaps increase its magnitude in areas which are less easily observed or controlled.

The principle of proportionality has a powerful presence throughout government, especially in the UK, an issue which divides it from the ways in which decision-making are often made within systems of government in European neighbours and which have a strong influence within the European Commission. Proportionality, or risk-based decision-making, is most obviously manifest within rules-based decision-making underpinned by economic impact assessments. In the UK, these are codified within the Treasury Green Book (HM Treasury 2018a). This is a highly developed process for assessing the risk involved with policy decisions by building evidence to assess the best option in each case. The process of adaptive management is also encoded in these procedures because decisions are also supposed to be accompanied by evaluation of the outcomes as they evolve, and in the UK, these are encoded in the Magenta Book (HM Treasury 2018b).

A criticism of this process is that it is based on a system of pseudo-quantified economic analysis – where most of the important considerations are given a financial cost. Many would agree that costing all variables in a complex set of considerations, especially moral considerations, is not feasible, so some of these procedures lack realism and, therefore, create an impression of certainty and objectivity where there is really very large uncertainty. Rather than mitigating risk, this process can create new risk by building an unjustified belief in the risk assessment process itself.

The risk of disasters

No government should ever be off its guard. Aleatory risks lurk around every corner, and governments need to be prepared for the next disaster. These kinds of risks are by their very nature unpredictable, often high impact and difficult to manage. Earthquakes, volcanoes, and floods are common examples, but these would also include challenges such as nuclear disasters and terrorism events. By definition they include all the kinds of events we cannot predict. A highly structured mechanism is needed to ensure that these risks are managed effectively. In the UK, this involves two strands.

First, there is a national risk assessment which supports a national risk register. This examines the various broad classes of risks which could affect the country. In general, the kind of risks which appear on the risk register are those which require the mobilisation of national assets to control them and which would involve multiple departments of state. The assessments have the benefit of capturing the generic national risks and allocating responsibility across government for the management of those risks.

One of the interesting features of these risk registers is their propensity to redefine aleatory risks as epistemic risks – governments are profoundly uncomfortable about aleatory risk, but this propensity for redefinition is itself a risk because it can create a false sense of security. The more generalised the definitions of risks within these national risk registers, the more likely they are to cope with aleatory forms of risk.

Second, there is the centralised infrastructure and processes used in response to a risk turning into a real event. This is probably not the place to describe this in detail, but it involves firm top-down command and control which can be mobilised within minutes of an event happening, such as a terrorist incident. Slower moving events, like those associated with infectious disease, use the same procedures but involving slightly different pre-defined people and infrastructure. Science advice is a very important, integrated part of the response procedures.

Broadly, these two strands represent 'preparation' and 'response', respectively. A third strand involves 'recovery' which can include long-term repair associated with physical damage, contamination, or psychological stress. An additional feature of the preparation is the simulation of real events which exercises the response capabilities. These involve attempting to understand the dynamics of decision-making, and the performance of the command and control structure when both are stressed. A common feature learned from the management of many of these kinds of risks, both real and simulated, is that rapid and highly coordinated action is vital to help contain the problem and to stop the risk mushrooming out of control.

Conclusion

Government decision-making is designed around risk management. There is an immutable relationship between risk management culture and the process of government. Government risk is offset by innovation and entrepreneurship, including innovation in policy and administration as well as technology and markets. This always has two faces – one involving risk mitigation and management, and the other involving amplifying risk – which need to be balanced. Risk management around decision-making in government is highly codified in some areas, but in others it relies on the intuition and experience of government managers to judge the level of risk which is acceptable in any particular circumstance. A capacity to capture strategic risks to design out risk over the long term and to build risk management into the business processes around structured decision-making in government is key to successful risk management. For example, decisions about investments by government in the UK at all levels now need to factor the risks from climate change (O'Connor, Bord & Fisher 1999) into decisions, and soon this will be accompanied by issues such as natural capital and resource conservation.

However, perhaps the greatest challenge for risk management in any government comes when deciding where to set its risk appetite. Few governments do this explicitly, but it would be good if they did and new mechanisms are needed to help governments understand their aggregate risk liability and how this should be priced. Democratic governments are generally very risk averse because the political consequences of even quite small risks materialising as real and adverse outcomes can magnify non-linearly. This unpredictability about how risks can magnify – sometimes termed social amplification (Kasperson et al. 1988; Lofstedt 2008; Pidgeon & Henwood 2010) – is a feature of democracies in developed counties with high standards of press freedom. But it would probably be misguided of governments to imagine that the control of this kind of risk comes about through strong risk aversion and, therefore, by setting a low level of risk tolerance. The irruptive nature of risk manifestation is more likely to be linked to trust (Lofstedt 2005; Poortinga & Pidgeon 2003) in those in charge. Ironically, and perhaps counter-intuitively, those governments which have a strong aversion to risk resulting in a culture of control are likely to be less trusted, will bring upon themselves greater costs, and are, therefore, more likely to suffer from the dual disadvantage of unpredictable risk amplification and loss of the advantages which accrue from innovation which happens when there is a high tolerance of risk.

References

Barth, JR, Caprio, G & Levine, R 2002, 'Bank regulation and supervision: what works best?', *Journal of Financial Intermediation*, vol. 13, pp. 205–248.

Boyd, Ian L 2016, 'Take the long view', *Nature*, vol. 540, no. 7634, p. 520. doi:10.1038/540520a.

Brulle, RJ & Pellow, DN 2006, 'Environmental justice: human health and environmental inequalities', *Annual Review of Public Health*, vol. 27, pp. 103–124.

Burke, MB et al. 2009, Warming increases the risk of civil war in Africa. *Proceedings of the National Academy of Science of the United States of America*, vol. 106, pp. 20670–20674.

Cabinet Office 2017, *Guidance: management of risk in government: framework.* Available from: www.gov.uk/government/publications/management-of-risk-in-government-framework.

Centers for Disease Control and Prevention (CDC). Hierarchy of Controls U.S. National Institute for Occupational Safety and Health. Retrieved [31 January 2017].

Diebold, FX 2006, 'Forecasting the term structure of government bond yields', *Journal of Econometrics*, vol. 130, pp. 337–364.

European Commission 2000, *Communication from the Commission on the Precautionary Principle.* Brussels: European Commission, (COM 2000–1 Final).

European Environment Agency 2001, Late lessons from early warnings: the precautionary principle 1896–200. Luxembourg: Office for Official Publications of the European Communities, 2001. ISBN 92-9167-323-4.

Galtier, F 2013, 'Managing food price instability: critical assessment of the dominant doctrine', *Global Food Security – Agriculture, Policy, Economics and Environment*, vol. 2, pp. 72–81.

Godfray, HCJ, Donnelly, CJ, Kao, RR, Macdonald, DW, McDonald, RA, Petrokofsky, G, Wood, JLN, Woodroffe, R, Young, DG & McLean, AR 2013, A restatement of the natural science evidence base relevant to the control of bovine tuberculosis in Great Britain. *Proceedings of the Royal Society B*, vol. 280. doi:10.1098/rspb.2013.1634.

Government Office for Science 2014, Innovation: Managing Risk, Not Avoiding It. *Annual Report of the Government Chief Scientific Adviser 2014*. The Government Office for Science, London.

Government Office for Science 2018, Future of the sea: final report. www.gov.uk/government/publications/future-of-the-sea--2.

HM Treasury 2013, The orange book: management of risk principles and concepts. Available from: www.gov.uk/government/publications/orange-book.

HM Treasury 2018a, The green book: appraisal and evaluation in central government. Available from: www.gov.uk/government/publications/the-green-book-appraisal-and-evaluation-in-central-governent. ISBN 978-1-912225-57-6.

HM Treasury 2018b, The magenta book: guidance for evaluation. Available from: www.gov.uk/government/publications/the-magenta-book.

Kasperson, RE, Renn, O, Slovic, P, Brown, HS, Emel, J, Goble, R, Kasperson, JX & Ratick, S 1988, The social amplification of risk a conceptual framework. *Risk Analysis*, vol. 8, pp. 177–187.

Larkin, J 2003, 'Strategic reputational risk management', *Palgrave Macmillan UK*, vol. 276. doi: 10.1057/9780230511415.

Lofstedt, RE 2005, *Risk management in post trust societies*. Basingstoke: Palgrave Macmillan.

Lofstedt, RE 2008, 'Risk communication, media amplification and the aspartame scare', *Risk Management*, vol. 10, no. 4, pp. 257–284.

Lofstedt, R 2011, 'Risk versus hazard – how to regulate in the 21st century', *European Journal of Risk Regulation*, vol. 2, no. 2, pp. 149–168.

Lofstedt, R. 2014. 'The precautionary principle in the EU: why a review is long overdue', *Risk Management*, vol. 16, pp. 137–163. doi.org/10.1057/rm.2014.7.

Maystadt, JF, Tan, JFT & Breisinger, C 2014, 'Does food security matter for transition in Arab countries?', *Food Policy*, vol. 46, pp. 106–115.

O'Connor, RE, Bord, RJ & Fisher, A 1999, 'Risk perceptions, general environmental beliefs, and willingness to address climate change', *Risk Analysis*, vol. 19, pp. 461–471.

Pidgeon, N & Henwood, K 2010, 'The Social Amplification of Risk Framework (SARF): theory, critiques, and policy implications', in *Risk communication and public health*, eds. Bennett, P. et al. Oxford Scholarship online. doi: 10.1093/acprof:oso/9780199562848.003.04.

Poortinga, W & Pidgeon NF 2003, 'Exploring the dimensionality of trust in risk regulation', *Risk Analysis*, vol. 23, pp. 961–972.

Rodrik, D 1998, 'Why do more open economies have bigger governments?', *Journal of Political Economy*, vol. 106, pp. 997–1032.

Sitkin, SB & Pablo, AL 1992, 'Reconceptualizing the determinants of risk behaviour', *Academy of Management Review*, vol. 17, pp. 9–38.

Urquhart, J, Potter, C, Barnett, J, Fellenor, J, Mumford, J & Quine, CP 2017, 'Expert perceptions and the social amplification of risk: a case study in invasive tree pests and disease', *Environmental Science and Policy*, vol. 77, pp. 172–178.

Weber, EU 2006, Experience-based and description-based perceptions of long-term risk: why global warming does not scare us (yet). *Workshop on Global Warming – The Psychology of Long Term Risk*. Princeton University, Princeton NJ, November 12, 2004.

Weinstein, ND & Klein, WM 1996, 'Unrealistic optimism: present and future', *Journal of Social and Clinical Psychology*, vol. 15, pp. 1–8. doi: 10.1521/jscp.1996.15.1.1.

World Health Organization. 2015, Antimicrobial resistance. Fact sheet N°194 www.who.int/en/news-room/fact-sheets/detail/antimicrobial-resistance access-date=24 February 2018.

5   The handling of uncertainty

A risk manager's perspective

Geoffrey Podger

The purpose of this chapter is to consider the handling of uncertainty from the point of view *not* of the risk assessor but rather from that of the risk manager and risk communicator. I can claim some authority in this area having myself spent rather more years than I care to remember in these two capacities in the areas of food safety and workplace health and safety. In particular, I would like to comment on the European Food Safety Authority (EFSA)'s new guidance on uncertainty from this perspective as I think this has been rather neglected for reasons I will try and explain and with potentially very damaging consequences. The first point to stress is the importance of covering uncertainty in risk assessments and not seeking to hide away the points of doubt. This has a particular resonance for those of us engaged in food safety post-bovine spongiform encephalopathy (BSE) when it became clear that the Southwood Committee had made a major assumption without supporting evidence that BSE might be expected to behave like scrapie and not "jump the species barrier" to humans. What they had done to reach their conclusion was to make a judgement in the absence of evidence—in itself a perfectly legitimate process but one which needed to have the surrounding doubts fully explained rather than simply say that if they were wrong "the implications would be extremely serious". The consequence was that what struck in the public mind about Southwood was not this very important qualification but rather the reassurance to be repeated over and over that "it was most unlikely that BSE will have implications for human health". Sadly history was to show otherwise!

The subsequent BSE inquiry, which produced by general consent a very measured view of the epidemic and its handling, stated in my view wholly correctly that "throughout the BSE story the approach to communication of risk was shaped by a consuming fear of provoking an irrational public scare". Indeed during the subsequent period when I was about to become Chief Executive of the Food Standards Agency (FSA), I remember vividly a discussion based on exactly the same faulty premise. It had become fashionable for the media to torment Ministers and public officials as to whether they could guarantee that various aspects of the food chain were "perfectly safe" and faced with the same fear guarantees had been given in terms which those responsible must have known were untrue. In the discussion in question the newly appointed Chair of the FSA, the immensely able Lord Krebs, made clear that the FSA would refuse to make such claims and make clear that "perfect safety" could never be guaranteed and that the issue was rather whether controls and products now met acceptable standards. It was clear from the reaction to this that the general view of Whitehall colleagues was that the FSA would be lucky to last a week—yet the FSA comprehensively followed Lord Krebs's approach, public confidence in the food supply was restored, and the FSA is happily still standing 16 years later. There is, however, a need to be careful not to interpret what I have just said as indicating that risk managers and communicators have carte blanche in how they present the scientific uncertainties inherently contained in the risk assessment. In particular risk managers and communicators have to be ready to face hostile stakeholders and media on controversial issues and to persuade others who have not been part of the risk assessment process to play their role in this. Tricky!

I remember as Executive Director of EFSA facing considerable unpopularity both from the Commission and from interested stakeholder groups over the judgements we made on the safety of genetically modified organisms (GMOs). These consisted of attacks on the science, and when these were unsuccessful attacks on the scientists involved in highly unfair and prejudicial terms. EFSA was able to deal with this by publishing clear and open opinions, and by religiously and fairly examining supposed "new evidence", even where it was arguably a priori of a very questionable kind. It also engaged personally with interested stakeholders, and I remember in particular the conversation which I had with an anti-GMO stakeholder who said to me— with commendable honesty if nothing else—that whatever we said on safety, his organization would never change its view! Even worse was the newspaper reporter who claimed to me in a private discussion that they had a contractual obligation to start two food scares a month! The point of these anecdotes is simply to make the point that we cannot take the view that either opposed stakeholders or the media will simply take scientific statements of uncertainty objectively or in context. I have no doubt that the risk assessor/communicator who does not prepare against this eventuality will quickly be doomed. Indeed officials and politicians who will find themselves explaining decisions made in the face of significant uncertainties will need a lot of convincing that they are on sure ground before being prepared to articulate and support decisions which are perfectly justified on the scientific evidence—uncertainties included!

Moving on specifically to the EFSA guidance I have already indicated that it is to be welcomed in terms of improving risk assessment. This, however, leaves unanswered the question as to what effect it will have on risk management and risk communication. Indeed EFSA's own position on this seems to be that the risk management implications are for the risk managers (i.e., the Commission) and that the risk communication consequences are being dealt with by a separate working party. This illustrates to my mind a significant risk in the whole exercise and a consequence of how EFSA was created since it was separated from the risk managers as a source of independent advice, and at the same time the whole risk analysis system created was supposed to have the task of "promoting coherence between the risk assessment, risk management and risk communication functions". In my view the present EFSA exercise is not going to be helpful in achieving that objective, and I think the reasons are clear. The risk managers are going to find themselves confronted with both an opinion recommending one thing and a detailed annex explaining why this may be untrue because of the uncertainties involved. Moreover the manner in which these uncertainties are expressed is not likely to be comprehensible to most, if not almost all, risk managers unless they are experts in mathematics, and unlike this audience unlikely to understand the references to "Bayesian modelling methodologies", "probability bounds analysis" or my favourite example "posterior distribution". The fact that the guidance comes to over 200 pages is not in my view inspiring of confidence. This is not of course to argue that sophisticated statistical techniques should not be used in producing EFSA opinions but rather that we are moving away from EFSA's responsibility to its interested public if opinions can only be understood by scientists working in the field. Having more generally intelligible summaries alone is in my view not the answer to this as a summary cannot convey the full weight of an opinion. Moreover, the new statements of uncertainty will clearly be a godsend to those who have reasons of their own for wishing to dispute particular opinions as they will now have a separate takeaway to use out of context consisting simply of objections to the opinion.

A nightmare for risk communicators as can be seen from the Melamine worked example given by the Scientific Committee which to a layman would simply cast doubt on the value of the opinion. So, we have the dilemma: it is right to improve the identification of uncertainties in risk assessment, but doing so in isolation risks devaluing the credibility of risk assessments and thus the reliance of risk managers and communicators on them. This then will play into the hands of those who wish to dispute the opinion not on scientific grounds (which is a legitimate debate in the public interest) but rather through misrepresentation and oversimplification of the arguments. We must also be alert to the risk that risk assessors will become less risk averse. Risk assessors in my experience are to their credit properly wary of rushing to judgement on controversial issues whether the controversy is scientific or populist or both. No one wants to be proven wrong in such circumstances. However, under the new EFSA system, they will always be able to point to some obscure table in the uncertainty annex as the justification of their position rather than have to necessarily confront the full implications of such issues in their decision. Is there then an answer? I think so and simply stated it is that if we are for good reason to give more attention to the uncertainties in an opinion, then we have to put these uncertainties in context and explain in generally comprehensible terms why the conclusions of the opinion are nevertheless the right ones on present knowledge. This seems to me an important exercise in its own right for both risk managers and communicators since, having undertaken such an uncertainty analysis as is now proposed, they may well wish/need to revise their opinion anyway—a very valuable exercise. It would also provide decision-makers and risk communicators with clear and hopefully persuasive arguments for acting on the opinions. If we want scientific evidence to play its full part in decision-making it seems to me nothing else will do.

So to conclude, based on my experience as a risk manager and communicator: (1) we should not be afraid of further development of work on scientific uncertainty in scientific risk assessments; (2) we should not take the view that the public cannot cope with uncertainty—as Dame Louise Casey has said more than once "the public are not stupid"; (3) conversely, we have to realize that extensive further discussion of uncertainty in isolation will result in providing undesirable assistance for those who wish to discredit the evidence for purposes of their own unrelated to science, and will reduce the will of decision-makers and communicators to defend them; and (4) the way forward therefore is for risk assessments to both state uncertainties more fully **and** plainly explain why the opinion is nevertheless valid on present knowledge. This approach seems to me the only way we can both serve the interests of scientific debate and of the man in the street whose interests at the end of the day all regulators are there to serve.

Index

Printed in the United States
by Baker & Taylor Publisher Services